JOHN SLOAN 1871-1951

JOHN SLOAN

1871–1951

HIS LIFE AND PAINTINGS *David W. Scott*
HIS GRAPHICS *E. John Bullard*

BOSTON BOOK & ART, PUBLISHER   BOSTON

NATIONAL GALLERY OF ART   WASHINGTON

Library of Congress Catalog Card Number 76-158452

SBN 8435-2026-4

Designed by Hubert Leckie, Washington

Composition by Harlowe Typography, Inc., Washington

Produced by Eastern Press, Inc., New Haven

PREFACE AND ACKNOWLEDGMENTS

J. Carter Brown, Director, National Gallery of Art

THE AMERICAN PAINTER AND GRAPHIC ARTIST John Sloan was born in Lock Haven, Pennsylvania in 1871. The National Gallery of Art has chosen the centennial anniversary of his birth to present a review of his richly varied activity. This is the seventh in a series of exhibitions honoring important American artists. In the past, the work of George Bellows, Winslow Homer, Thomas Eakins, John Singleton Copley, Gilbert Stuart, and Mary Cassatt has been the subject of similar presentations.

We are fortunate to have as associates in this project five museums—the Georgia Museum of Art, the De Young Memorial Museum, the City Art Museum of St. Louis, the Columbus Gallery of Fine Arts and the Pennsylvania Academy of the Fine Arts,—who, by bringing the exhibition to widely different parts of the country, make this truly a national centennial celebration. I would like to thank the directors and staffs of these institutions for their participation and cooperation.

Yearly, as exhibitions become more difficult to mount, I am increasingly aware of the crucial role the lender, particularly the private lender, plays in making it possible to honor properly an artist such as John Sloan. To the collectors and museums who have so generously shared their pictures with us, I extend our sincere gratitude and appreciation.

I must express our special indebtedness to Helen Farr Sloan, the widow of the artist. All who know this extraordinary woman are impressed with her energy, scholarship, and warmth. Through her work at the Delaware Art Museum, which houses the Sloan Archives, and with graduate students at the University of Delaware and elsewhere, she has made an important contribution to our knowledge and appreciation of the work of John Sloan and his contemporaries. From the beginning Helen Sloan has cooperated with our staff in all details of the organization of this exhibition. For this we are most grateful.

Many others have been of great assistance. David W. Scott served as organizer of the exhibition, and E. John Bullard and Moussa Domit were Gallery curators in charge. Grant Holcomb, a former Kress Fellow, contributed to the listings in the catalog.

EXHIBITION DATES

NATIONAL GALLERY OF ART, Washington
September 18, 1971 through October 31, 1971

GEORGIA MUSEUM OF ART, Athens
November 20, 1971 through January 16, 1972

M. H. DE YOUNG MEMORIAL MUSEUM, San Francisco
February 15, 1972 through April 2, 1972

CITY ART MUSEUM OF ST. LOUIS
May 4, 1972 through June 18, 1972

COLUMBUS GALLERY OF FINE ARTS
July 13, 1972 through August 13, 1972

PENNSYLVANIA ACADEMY OF THE FINE ARTS, Philadelphia
September 6, 1972 through October 22, 1972

CONTENTS

LENDERS TO THE EXHIBITION

Addison Gallery of American Art, Phillips Academy, Andover
Herbert S. Alder, New York
Mr. and Mrs. Arthur G. Altschul, New York
Anonymous Lenders
Mr. and Mrs. L. H. Aricson, Philadelphia
Art Institute of Chicago
Mr. and Mrs. Philip Berman, Allentown
Bowdoin College Museum of Art, Brunswick
Mr. Julian Brodie, New York
The Brooklyn Museum
Canajoharie Library and Art Gallery, New York
Dr. and Mrs. Martin Cherkasky, Bronx
The Cleveland Museum of Art
Colorado Springs Fine Arts Center
The Columbus Gallery of Fine Arts
Corcoran Gallery of Art, Washington
Dartmouth College Collection, Hanover
Delaware Art Center, Wilmington
The Detroit Institute of Arts
Jo Ann and Julian Ganz, Los Angeles
Mr. Herbert A. Goldstone, New York
Joseph H. Hirshhorn Collection, New York
Mrs. John F. Kraushaar, New York
Miss Ruth Martin, New York
Mrs. Casimir B. Mayshark, Santa Fe
Memorial Art Gallery of the University of Rochester
The Metropolitan Museum of Art, New York
Milwaukee Art Center
Museum of Fine Arts, Boston
Museum of New Mexico, Santa Fe
National Collection of Fine Arts, Smithsonian Institution, Washington
National Gallery of Art, Washington
Parrish Art Museum, Southampton
Pennsylvania Academy of the Fine Arts, Philadelphia
Philadelphia Museum of Art
The Phillips Collection, Washington
Mr. and Mrs. Meyer Potamkin, Philadelphia
Mr. and Mrs. J. Warner Prins, New York
Dr. and Mrs. Harold Rifkin, Bronx
Dr. and Mrs. James Seaman, Durham
Sheldon Memorial Art Gallery, University of Nebraska, Lincoln
John Sloan Trust
Syracuse University
Wadsworth Atheneum, Hartford
Walker Art Center, Minneapolis
Whitney Museum of American Art, New York
Yale University Art Gallery, New Haven

FOREWORD

Helen Farr Sloan

When I was asked to express what this centennial exhibition means to me, and, something much more difficult, exactly what John Sloan thought about the future of his work—one idea came to my mind and now stays in my heart—an exhibition like this is the finest birthday present that can be given to an artist. It is a creative act which gives new life to an artist's lifework. The honor of a retrospective exhibition sponsored by our National Gallery of Art is a mark of recognition that the artist has made a contribution to America's cultural heritage which has stood the test of time.

This honor is not only a thing of words set in a book but it is expressed in the form of an exhibition. Only in this way, by assembling a comprehensive collection of the artist's pictures, can the paintings be seen in their complete integrity and diversity of character. Reproductions inevitably reduce the substance, change the scale, and compress the qualities of color orchestration. Sloan's work as a drafts-man can be known through the prints and drawings. In painting, he was concerned with the problem of style that is "hidden under the cloak of representation." His work, and that of any colorist when the pictures exist in many separate places, remains only partially understood. The variety of concepts within an artist's oeuvre, the relationship to brother-artists of the past and the contemporary generation—these factors cannot be evaluated without the opportunity which such an exhibition provides. This opportunity to judge the work is not only for the experts, but it is here to be shared with all who come to see it.

I think that Sloan would want me to report his ideas about realism and the notion that representational art is merely a kind of photographic image that passes rapidly through the artist's imagination and emerges on the canvas in hard or soft edge, colored, oil paint. Anyone who heard him teach must remember the ringing sound of his voice, saying: "The camera is only a machine; it has no mind, no conscience, no heart. It has no memory. It is blind." A few minutes later, he would pick up another thread of this thought: "Draw what you know about life, about reality. The deep-seated truths that a blind man knows about existence. When the model is in front of you, draw as though you were working from memory. There is a human being, with a soul. Draw with kindness, graciousness. It is only too easy to draw with cruelty, to express the things you dislike. Real art cannot be made out of negative ideas. Find something that interests you in life, that is worthwhile talking about. The reason an artist uses the graphic language is because he has something to say about order, truth, goodness, and what he finds beautiful—something that cannot be expressed in words."

That is how I remember John Sloan speaking, and what I have here written is based on notes made the first day I heard him teach at the Art Students League in October, 1927. He took every opportunity to teach others to find the way to be happy in their own work, with their own kind of talent. He looked forward to a new renaissance of culture in this country of two hundred million souls. He hoped that labor-saving machinery would provide leisure time for creative work in all the arts. He looked on the field of culture as a garden where many kinds of talent should flourish at the same time, saying that there should be room for work in every style. He understood the importance of what is the ecology of culture, and raised his voice against the dangers of inbreeding, parasitism of art on art. He encouraged growth and change and a man's urge to experiment; yet he was wise enough to know, as do the scientists, that not all changes or mutations are good. It was his particular concern to guard against that kind of accidental censorship which might crush the initiative of fresh and new-born talents, in times when fashions or ideologies in culture tend to ignore or discourage what is not considered avant garde. "We do not know where the new great talents are coming from, when or where they will be born. The modern Giotto may be a baby today, in Brooklyn or some village in South Dakota. It takes time for an artist to grow up. He needs the opportunity to study, to mature in his own way."

There is yet another kind of birthday gift for the artist represented in this fine catalog which sets the memory of the exhibition in permanent form. The essays by scholars draw a picture of the man and his work from a different perspective. In these notes I have tried to let Sloan speak for himself wherever possible, but the reproductions also communicate what he had to say, in the language of images, which is the medium he chose when his ideas could not be expressed in words. He would be most grateful that this book-length catalog is handsome in format, but he would be even more so that its moderate price should make it available to many people.

I hope it has been possible to read between the lines of what I have written about the meaning of this exhibition. As wife and widow of a man like John Sloan I know that there must be a patient time of waiting for history to test a man's work: during his lifetime, immediately after, later, and then again. Sloan and I talked about this together, but neither of us ever set up any goals in terms of time or place by which to measure what the test of time really means. History is made by real people, whose actions cannot be predicted. In the case of art, it is made by the artists and the consumers of art who like that art and the critics who are trained scholars of it.

This exhibition, which dispels the ashcan myth, dusting off Sloan's memory, putting his work in its true light and setting his philosophy of life free from distortion—the whole planning of this creative project with its quiet elegance—would have touched him very much. For while he was silent when most serious, we might hear him saying now to all the scholars and administrators and friends who have helped in the preparation of this catalog and this exhibition, "Thank you—all of you!"

John Sloan and Helen Farr Sloan in their Hotel Chelsea studio,
New York City, 1950.
Colten Photograph

I am a realist, working in the tradition of Daumier,
Courbet, Rembrandt and Carpaccio. I am more interested
in the noble commonplace of nature than in the curious:
believing that form and color are tools of the artist's
imagination in re-creating life.

John Sloan, quoted in Helen Farr Sloan's diary, June 22, 1950

JOHN SLOAN: HIS LIFE AND PAINTINGS

David W. Scott

I

THE READER OF THIS CATALOG may well ask, "Who was the man John Sloan? What did he do? What was his art like? And what does this exhibition represent?"

We may begin with a sketch biography. John Sloan was born in 1871 in Lock Haven, Pennsylvania, a lumbering town where his Scotch Presbyterian forebears had been cabinet makers for generations. In 1876 his family moved to Philadelphia, closer to his mother's relatives, who were of English Episcopalian background and related by marriage to Marcus Ward, the English publisher. The youngster grew up in the world of fine books and illustrations and was an avid reader.

John Sloan entered Philadelphia's Central High School in the same class as William Glackens and Albert C. Barnes (who later established the Barnes Foundation). When he was sixteen his father failed in business and Sloan left school to work to help support the family. He took a position as assistant cashier in a firm that dealt in books, greeting cards and fine prints, and he found time to continue his reading (he especially enjoyed Dickens, Balzac and Zola) and also to make greeting cards on his own.

Before long he taught himself etching and developed enough skill in drawing and lettering to win himself a job in a fancy goods business, from which he went on to try his fortune as a free lance artist. Commissions proving unpredictable, in 1892 he joined the staff of the Philadelphia *Inquirer*.

The character of the stubborn, struggling youngster was well described in a letter of recommendation written at about this time by his uncle, William H. Ward, to the manager of the Philadelphia Engraving Company:

> S. S. Teutonic
> 23rd Nov., 1891
>
> *. . . He is very assiduous in evening study at Art Classes, and I feel sure that he has decided talent and will get on. One good trait in his character is his independence. He has got along so far entirely unassisted, and is determined to rely upon his own labor in the future, and also to help his mother. This makes the earning of some steady sum, small though it may be for a time, a necessity; and may retard the rapidity of his progress in art—but with determination to get on he is sure to succeed in the long run. . . .*

The nineties were the heyday of the newspaper illustrators, and dozens of young Philadelphia artists worked on staffs of the various papers until the process of photomechanical reproduction displaced them. Thus it was that Sloan entered into a lively world of art when he joined the *Inquirer* staff: not only was his immediate superior the sympathetic art director and painter E. Wyatt Davis (father of Stuart Davis), but Sloan's other associates came to include William Glackens, George Luks, Everett Shinn, James Preston and George Fox. Though these artists never worked together on one paper at one time, most of them sooner or later served on the Philadelphia *Press*, where Sloan himself worked from 1895 to 1903.

The newspaper artists were closely associated with the Pennsylvania Academy and its younger alumni and teachers. Sloan attended Thomas Anshutz' Antique Class in 1892 and 1893, and he also became a close friend of Robert Henri, who had returned to Philadelphia after capping his work at the Academy with several years of study in Paris. Sloan soon frequented Henri's studio, which became a gathering place for younger artists who listened to inspired, impromptu lectures from their dynamic host when not engaging in exuberant amateur theatricals.

Beginning in 1895, Sloan's friends—including Henri, Glackens, Luks and Shinn—began to leave Philadelphia, eventually settling in New York. Sloan had already achieved a certain national recognition as one of the leading artists of the poster style, and his job of producing decorative headings and illustrations held him at the paper until 1903. By that time the day of the newspaper artist was almost over, and Sloan's work for the *Press* was reduced to a weekly word charade puzzle. In the spring of 1904 he went to New York to try to earn his living as a free-lance illustrator.

On this move he was accompanied by his young wife, Dolly, the former Anna M. Wall, a diminutive, spirited Irish girl he had married in 1901. Sloan arrived in the city with few prospects for work, and for several years he had to walk the rounds of the magazine offices regularly to get enough commissions so that he and Dolly could live, but they found New York enormously stimulating and soon they were surrounded by friends. They moved to a "garret," a small fifth floor apartment on West Twenty-third Street, and Sloan began to soak in the rich human comedy that surrounded him.

Meanwhile, his old friend William Glackens had found him a thoroughly challenging commission. The Frederick J. Quinby Company had undertaken to issue the collected

works of the minor French novelist Charles Paul de Kock in deluxe illustrated editions. Although the project was to prove overambitious as a publishing venture, it afforded Sloan the opportunity to create his first major set of illustrations, lively depictions of the French social scene of the earlier nineteenth century.

As his work for Quinby drew to a close in 1905, Sloan carried on full tilt with etchings of New York scenes, creating a set of ten City Life prints. They won critical acclaim, but when he took them by invitation to the American Water Color Society's exhibition in April of 1906, the hanging committee declared that four of the set were too vulgar for public display. Sloan's indignation subsequently turned to a deep disappointment as he found great difficulty in finding purchasers.

Equally discouraging for Sloan was the lack of public interest when he attempted to sell his paintings, although the critics and even the juries often endorsed his work. He was first included in major shows in 1900, and during

the following decade he exhibited frequently at the Pennsylvania Academy, the Carnegie Institute and the National Academy of Design.

Along with acceptances came rejections. Juries disagreed over the merits of the work of painters of the Henri circle, and on several occasions the painters suffered complete rebuffs, while on others they found their work "skied" or hung in obscure corners. Though friendly critics praised their freshness of approach, hostile reviewers attacked them for lack of finish, vulgarity and unhealthiness (that is, lack of conventional beauty).

It was after a particularly sharp disagreement with members of a National Academy jury on which he served that Henri announced, in the spring of 1907, that he and his friends would hold an exhibition in the Macbeth Gallery in February, 1908. The old Philadelphia gang— Henri, Sloan, Glackens, Luks and Shinn—was joined by Arthur B. Davies, Maurice Prendergast and Ernest Lawson. The newspapers dramatized the announcement

The studio at 806 Walnut Street, Philadelphia, c. 1895. George Luks is the "boxer" with his head lowered; behind him, left to right, are James Preston, John Sloan and Everett Shinn. *Sloan Collection, Delaware Art Museum*

by reporting that The Eight (as they were dubbed) were challenging the Academy, though the artists themselves regarded their venture as an attempt to broaden exhibition opportunities, not as a break with the Establishment. The show's colorful press coverage helped make it a sensational success—it was heavily attended and even well patronized, although Sloan, as usual, sold nothing. National interest was aroused and the paintings (with a few replacements) were sent off on a tour around the country.

Sloan was in the thick of the arrangements, helping with the accounts, the catalog and the itinerary for the traveling show. We may see him at this period through the lively pages of the diary he kept (now published as *John Sloan's New York Scene*) and through articles that began to appear on his work, such as one written by Charles Wisner Barrell for *The Craftsman,* February, 1909:

John Sloan is classed as a member of what is known in academic

circles as the "Revolutionary Gang" or the "Black School" . . . . He has made his home in the heart of New York City in a picturesque top-story den on West Twenty-third Street, just on the outskirts of the seething Tenderloin. New York to him is America crystallized, and from his roof or studio window he can watch the pageant of humanity stream by in all its million phases.

In 1910 Sloan again joined with members of the Henri group (including some of the promising Henri students) in staging the Exhibition of Independent Artists, which caused a sensation even surpassing that of the Macbeth show. After this venture, the leadership of the more advanced art movement slipped from Henri personally. In the case of the next major independent exhibition, the Armory Show of 1913, Arthur B. Davies became the principal organizer. Sloan helped hang the show and was represented in it, but his role was in fact relatively minor.

Sloan once recalled—making a point by overstatement— that during his newspaper days, he and his friends "knew nothing of world troubles." When he went to New York, he

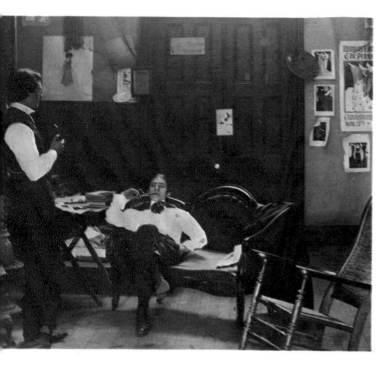

John Sloan (left) and Joe Laub in their studio at 806 Walnut Street, Philadelphia, 1895. *Sloan Collection, Delaware Art Museum*

Dolly Sloan, New York City, c. 1904-1906. *Sloan Collection, Delaware Art Museum*. Photograph by John Sloan.

sought to capture the whole gamut of the social scene, not to preach reform but to convey the vital pulse he felt everywhere. He was increasingly troubled, nevertheless, by signs of corruption and injustice. He dropped in at night courts and "boiled inwardly" at the "snap justice" dispensed there. In the fall of 1908 he was disillusioned by the election of Taft. During the following year he was well on the way to becoming a Socialist. He found himself a great admirer of Eugene Debs, but he could not follow Henri's enthusiasm for the anarchist Emma Goldman.

In July of 1909 Sloan met John Butler Yeats, the Irish painter and philosopher, father of William Butler Yeats. The kindly old man, who soon became a very close friend, deplored the Socialist fever that seized John and Dolly at this time, but for three years the Sloans spent as much energy on Socialist Party matters as on art, until Sloan took a studio in the spring of 1912 and threw himself back into painting.

However, in 1912 Sloan began one last chapter of Socialist activity, for in that year he became an editor of the revamped *The Masses*. He was soon involved in new concepts of magazine layout and produced the most inspired graphic art of his career. He had determined that his role was to convey life as he saw it, not party propaganda, and after two years of brilliant (and voluntary) service, he began to withdraw from the periodical.

With the advent of World War I in 1914, he found the Socialist Party ineffectual in the face of the impending tragedy. He became increasingly disillusioned, and to the end of his life, while always holding liberal sympathies, he was skeptical of all governments and systems of reform.

After the Macbeth Gallery exhibition of 1908, Sloan began to receive more commissions as an illustrator. In January, 1909, he wrote in his diary that he had "taken in about $2750" during the preceding year—a sum that was "satisfactory" at a time when apartments could be rented for $50 a month and restaurants served full meals for a quarter. The Sloans lived modestly but comfortably, and in spite of some ups and downs and the fact that few paintings sold (Sloan's first sale did not occur until 1913, when he was forty-two), they eventually found adequate studio apartments that they could afford. From 1914 to 1918 they summered in Gloucester, where Sloan painted scores of fresh, direct canvases. Beginning in 1919, they went regularly to Santa Fe, which became a true second home for them, as they entered into community affairs and explored a new land. John Sloan, unlike the others of his circle, never traveled abroad, but he found the surviving Indian and Mexican cultures of the Southwest an education in the values of tradition.

After Sloan leased the loft studio in 1912, he began to take private students, and during his summers in

John Sloan, posing as Edgar Allan Poe, standing before one of the mural panels painted for the Pennsylvania Academy of the Fine Arts. February, 1897. *Sloan Collection, Delaware Art Museum*

Gloucester he became yet more heavily involved in teaching. Finally, in 1916, he joined the faculty of the Art Students League, and subsequently his principal source of livelihood was teaching rather than illustrating.

It was at about this time that he assumed the role which made him such a familiar public figure for more than a generation. He began exhibiting regularly, holding one-man shows at the Whitney Studio Club and the Kraushaar Galleries; he became president for life of the Society of Independent Artists; and he grew into a living tradition at the Art Students League. His students (a hardy, devoted group who could withstand his sharp tongue) included Otto Soglow, Peggy Bacon, Don Freeman, Edmund Duffy, Alexander Calder, David Smith, Angna Enters, Reginald Marsh, Doris Rosenthal, Aaron Bohrod, Lee Gatch, John Graham, George L. K. Morris, Adolph Gottlieb and Barnett Newman. In 1931 he was elected president of the League, but differences with other members of the Board led to his resignation in 1932. He taught briefly elsewhere, then returned until ill health forced his retirement in 1938.

John Sloan, for all his jaunty spirit, suffered from more than his share of infirmities. Particularly vexing was the trouble with his eyesight which developed into dyplopia (double vision), a condition partly corrected by an operation in 1945. He was also subject to severe jaundice attacks, and it was only after three operations for an obstruction of the gall duct that he began to rebuild his strength in 1943.

Dolly, even more than John, was long subject to periods of severe illness. In intervals of good health she worked heroically for various causes—especially for the Socialist Party before the First World War, but also for community ventures in Santa Fe and as manager for the Gallery of American-Indian Art in New York. By 1940, however, she was again ill, and after a brief recovery she died of a coronary in May, 1943.

In February of the following year John married Helen Farr, an artist who had been a close friend of the Sloans since she had attended his League classes in the twenties. It was from her notes on his class discussions that she developed the text of his *Gist of Art* (1939).

Following his marriage to Helen Farr, John Sloan entered another vigorous phase in his painting. By 1945 he was fully recovered in health and stimulated by recognition that came to him from many quarters—though his current painting, as usual, failed to find ready appreciation. He lectured, socialized, prepared exhibitions, expressed himself freely to the press on a variety of subjects, and created some of the strongest pictures of his career.

As Sloan's eightieth birthday approached, Lloyd Goodrich, director of the Whitney Museum, undertook preparations for a major retrospective. Goodrich characterized him vividly in the catalog he was preparing: "In his green old age, Sloan with his leonine mass of gray hair, his indomitable face, his keen eyes, and his sharp tongue, was one of the legendary characters of the art world." In preparation for the show, Sloan continued painting with his customary energy, but his doctors advised him not to return to the altitude of Santa Fe for the summer of 1951, so he went instead to Hanover, New Hampshire.

Sloan had not painted in New England since his Gloucester days more than thirty years before, and at first he felt "like a desert scorpion dropped into a green salad," but soon he was at work on six landscapes together. On August 2 he enjoyed a lively celebration of his eightieth birthday. Before the month was out, however, he learned he had a small cancer, and he underwent an operation which proved to have unexpectedly severe aftereffects. John Sloan died in the hospital at Hanover on the seventh of September, 1951.

John Sloan lives on not only through his art but through

the heritage of his dedicated activities. He was a selfless and immensely influential teacher; a tireless fighter for justice in a variety of causes; and a life-long champion of the liberalized exhibition opportunities which have by now afforded unprecedented encouragement to three generations of American artists.

II

JOHN SLOAN HAD A GIFT for incisive characterizations, expressing himself in aphorisms and telling visual images. In spite of his quickness of concept, as an artist he placed "solidity" or "realization" above facility and charm, and he was willing to work doggedly to achieve results he had in mind. His friends Henri, Glackens, Luks and Shinn were all men who made a display of their facility, but Sloan, after the early days in which he struggled for technical mastery, quite consciously resisted the effects of virtuosity. It was the struggle to convey a sense of reality that lay deeper than the paint surface that relates the first oils he exhibited in 1900 (nos. 19 and 20) to his last works of more than fifty years later.

Even before he began to paint regularly in oil, in the mid-nineties, Sloan had established himself as an artist of originality and talent, but in a very different vein. His calendars for A. Edward Newton (later a famous bibliophile) and his commercial posters led to decorative headings for the newspapers and to his being fully in the swing of the movement of the "poster period," which enjoyed great popularity from 1894 to 1896. Short-lived literary journals with posteresque covers appeared everywhere, and Sloan was briefly the art editor of a Philadelphia publication entitled *Moods*. He was recognized nationally as one of the leading artists of the poster style, no mean achievement for a young man of twenty-four who had received little art training and had matured slowly.

It was, in fact, only in 1895 that the drawing in Sloan's illustrations became assured and easy. In general, his poster period work is effective because of happily inventive composition and good craftsmanship rather than audacious flair, as in the case of his English and Continental counterparts. Nevertheless, the originality and skill of Sloan's work give it a secure place today in surveys of the style.

Some four years later Sloan helped develop a color printing process for use in the full page decorations he prepared for the Sunday supplement of the *Press*. His work shows great freedom, ease and imagination in the handling of form and color.

It was during the decade from 1895 to 1905 that Sloan first began to paint seriously in oil and worked into the manner of his first mature city life scenes (which became known as "Sloans.") Within this period, the earlier paintings often reflect the flat-patterning concern of his poster style and art nouveau illustrations (nos. 2, 20 and 22), but he worked progressively to capture the impression of the living reality of the scene, or of the tangible solidity of the model. His palette, like those of Henri and Glackens during the same years, was generally muted, running to blacks and neutrals with flashes of white and gleaming color.

After moving to New York and while preparing for the Macbeth Gallery exhibition of 1908, he came once again into the front rank of a major movement. The effectiveness of his characterizations of city life was such that it was Sloan, of the entire group of realists who encircled Henri as friends and students, who came to be regarded as typifying what was later, and somewhat misleadingly, termed the Ash Can School.

Almost simultaneously, John Sloan achieved recognition as one of the most original and forceful printmakers of the country. The ten etchings of his New York City Life set, dating from 1905 and 1906, shared with his paintings the force of freshly observed, warmly felt, directly expressed distillations of the New York milieu.

To see Sloan's achievement in proper perspective, we must recognize that he was not the first artist of the Henri circle to undertake a series of city life views (Shinn preceded him by several years); nor was he the most brutally realistic in characterization (Luks may claim that distinction). Furthermore, in the nineteenth century, city streets had been the subject of such painters as Childe Hassam and Louis Comfort Tiffany, while both Eakins and Anshutz provided precedents for the unvarnished depictions of everyday subjects. What Sloan did create was an idiom which allowed him to capture with great freshness and immediacy a wide variety of city life vignettes, alive with the human pulse he sensed all about him (nos. 36-51 and 53-58). On two scores he delighted some critics and enraged others: the relative looseness of his technique baffled those who equated realism with finish; and his wide range of episode ignored the classifications of good taste and vulgarity. The impressionists had shown that the city streets could be used as a subject if the treatment had charm, but Sloan rejected charm. He defied the categorization that made conservative viewers feel safely uninvolved: he moved back and forth from satire to sympathy, from high society to low life, in a way that was revolutionary at the time. Probably no other American painter has depicted the human comedy with such broadly-ranging humor and understanding.

Hardly had John Sloan made his mark as one of the leading painters of the New York scene, when he began to experiment in new techniques and subject matter. It was characteristic of him that his creative work came in waves, each with a shift of emphasis. "I have never been interested in painting or doing things I know I can paint or do," he said in the *Gist of Art.* "I get an attack of enthusiasm once in awhile that lasts me for several years."

In July of 1909 Sloan was introduced by Henri to Hardesty Maratta, who had prepared paints mixed to set color intervals. Sloan was soon experimenting with Maratta's pigments and his work took on a new richness of color. For the next twenty years he employed set palettes reflecting harmonies based on Maratta's theories.

Maratta also led Henri and Sloan into discussions of the rhythmic arrangement of pictorial elements. The pictorial language and building of form took on heightened importance to Sloan, who was beginning to feel limited by his city scene approach of casting about for a suitable episode or theme before beginning each picture (nos. 70 and 72).

The problem of determining the role subject matter should play was brought to a head by the experience of his Socialist "conversion," followed by the revelation of the Armory Show. For some years after Sloan joined the Socialist Party in January, 1910, he produced political cartoons, including some of his finest drawings, but he discovered that in proportion as he placed a conscious stress on subject matter he risked losing the sense of artistic truth as he knew it. To draw a spontaneous protest for the *The Masses,* such as his *Class War in Colorado* (no. 92)—was one thing; but to draw or paint propaganda, or even city life pictures, regularly as a program was quite another.

The Armory Show gave him the insight that the great tradition of painting, as a vital force, was still alive among the moderns and the "ultramoderns" (as he termed the more abstract artists), and that the search for realization could be carried on through daily work from

landscape or the figure more effectively than from sporadic painting of episodes. Even before the Armory Show, in 1912, he had taken a studio and begun to paint regularly from the model (no. 99). Subsequently, his summer paintings at Gloucester and then at Santa Fe allowed him to explore a wide variety of approaches, compositions and motives.

The first reflection in his work of the new movements revealed by the Armory Show appears to stem from van Gogh and the fauves—a freely-brushed, colorful and somewhat calligraphic approach in the Gloucester landscapes of 1914 and 1915 (nos. 104-6).

In the course of the summer of 1916, he began to place a strong emphasis on pictorial structure and the careful building of form (nos. 107-8). Indeed, these concerns were to remain uppermost for a number of years. To achieve firmer structure he employed such devices as the repressing of the foreground planes and tilting up of the background; stressing the principal geometric lines of the composition, and projecting horizontals, diagonals and verticals across the entire picture field; and on occasion treating the surface in somewhat geometricized planes (nos. 112, 115, 118, 120 and 136). These cubist-related devices remind us that as early as 1910 he had been intrigued by reproductions of Cézanne and after the Armory Show he became a friend of Marcel Duchamp;

however, by his own confession, he never painted an abstraction. The farthest point in his experimentation is represented by a half-serious, half-satirical etching and aquatint of 1917 entitled *Mosaic*.

The impact of this study of picture building may be traced through all his later work, where it appears, for example, in his resistance to visual perspective and, more generally, in his approach to form as a mental, not merely a visual, concept.

During the mid-twenties Sloan's probing of the questions of form was reflected particularly in his studies of nudes, carefully composed and modeled—indeed, sometimes quite masterful, but hardly radical in treatment (nos. 142-44). By late 1927 and 1928 he came to the conclusion that he could not carry his investigations further without modifying his technique (nos. 150-52). He began to use monochromatic underpainting followed by a superimposed color-textural glaze. Simultaneously, he became greatly interested in the corresponding under-

painting and glaze techniques of Renoir, Delacroix and Rembrandt, and in the form-building methods of these and other masters of the Western tradition.

In 1939, in the *Gist of Art,* he summarized the principles that governed his approach to painting after he adopted underpainting and glaze:

The importance of the mental technique of seeing things; an emphasis on plastic consciousness; the fact that all things in nature are composed of the five simple solids . . .; the significance of devices in drawing, by which we represent three-dimensional forms on a two-dimensional surface; the low relief concept of composition; the importance of foreshortening rather than visual perspective in signifying spacial projection and recession; the use of color as a graphic tool; emphasis on realization rather than realism as the essential quality of reality in art.

Thirty years earlier, Sloan had been content to say that he painted until he achieved solidity; now he conceived his goal as "realization" of the form of all parts of the figure and composition together. This meant the creation of an abstract formal order—"form as the mind knows it"—which included emphasis on tactile realization and suppression of perspective, going beyond the illusionistic. Indeed, it meant a conflict with the conventions of depicting visual appearances. This conflict led to a new crisis in the acceptance of his painting, but Sloan had never avoided conflict and the crisis strengthened his sense of independence.

Departing from visual representation was not itself anathema in 1928 or 1930. Sloan's first, freely brushed canvases in the underpainting technique (such as *Nude, Red Hair, Standing* (no. 150)—which relate easily to Glackens and Renoir—have great charm. But Sloan characteristically began to pose further problems for himself and to tackle them in an individualistic manner. In the course of this, he developed a method of describing form which struck many critics as inherently contradictory.

Nothing has caused more difficulty in the acceptance of Sloan's later work than his linear overlay or crosshatching, which may be viewed as the superimposition of an element foreign to our normal visual experience upon a painting order which derives from the visual world. To Sloan, whose years of drawing and etching made graphic linework second nature, it not only heightened the forms as visual and tactile symbols, but it helped transform the entire work to an experience on another level. He said that the "undersubstance is given realization by superimposed color-textures," and "texture is what vitalizes form."

Doctrinaire as the crosshatching appeared, Sloan was not fundamentally doctrinaire about method, though he was whole-heartedly committed to "realization" through the creation of vital bas-reliefs of sculptured form. Thus he sometimes carved away at monolithic figures (*Brunette Nude, Striped Blanket* no. 157) and sometimes used color texture to create a continuity of atmospheric effect (*Girl, Back to Piano* no. 160), often with Renoir in mind. Again, if forms developed properly without hachure, he let the pigmentation itself carry the impact (*Model in Dressing Room* and *Self-Portrait [Pipe and Brown Jacket]* nos. 161 and 168).

Since Sloan's approach after 1930 was broadly experimental, varying from painting to painting, we must evaluate his achievement on the basis of individual works. In a number of his pictures, his modulation of the superimposed textural statement does in fact accord with the total organization of form and color. His most

successful works attain to great richness, dignity and authority, and are at the same time thoroughly original.

John Sloan's first decade of experimentation in his new technique climaxed in the *Nude with Nine Apples* (1937, no. 165). The end of the thirties and early forties were trying years during which he could do little work, but in 1945 he entered into a culminating period of sustained, vigorous painting. He continued to work in tempera underpainting and oil and varnish glaze, with linear reinforcing, but his work of the last period goes

Santa Fe, Fiesta, 1932. John and Dolly Sloan are seated in the right foreground. Next to them are Amelia Elizabeth White and Gerald Cassidy. *Parkhurst Photograph*

form while restraining the chiaroscuro he had often employed in the thirties. The forms became larger, the planes broader and more carefully arranged, the colors simpler and more telling, the textural overlay more closely integrated into the whole. In the end, by a transformation of all pictorial elements together, he achieves his objective of carrying the observer beyond the world of superficial appearances to the world of concepts presented as tangible reality—a haunting, magic world, at once sensuous and austere, immediate and remote, present and timeless.

III

THE PRESENT SELECTION of the work of John Sloan seeks a balance between breadth and depth. Examples cover a span of over sixty years and include Sloan's achievements in the poster style, as an illustrator of newspapers, magazines and books, an etcher and art editor, a dedicated draftsman, and a painter of city scenes, landscapes, portraits and figure compositions.

There are here presented works that stand as signposts on Sloan's road: his first oil; the paintings he first exhibited in 1900 (*Walnut Street Theater* and *Independence Square, Philadelphia* nos. 19 and 20); the de Kock illustrations that preceded the New York city life scenes; figure and landscape studies reflecting his experiments before and after the Armory Show; his initial underpainting and glaze work in the late twenties; and, finally, an unfinished landscape from his last summer.

A special emphasis has been placed on what may be considered his characteristic achievements, those which exerted the most influence and those with which he is most closely associated. Thus, there are included all ten of the City Life set of etchings; all seven of the paintings exhibited at the historic Macbeth Gallery show of 1908; the two oils included in the Armory Show; long-time favorites such as *Back Yards, Greenwich Village* and views of McSorley's; richly glazed figure studies from the thirties; and examples of Sloan's culminating period, unfortunately still too little known.

The scope of John Sloan's activities as an artist is such that only through a survey of this extent can we grasp and appreciate the broad reach of his creative spirit.

further than his painting of the thirties and carries his experiments to a new synthesis.

"I feel that I must continue digging into this problem of drawing, the separation of form and color—the concept of the thing in its integrity, the realization of plastic existence. The problems which the artists of the early Renaissance solved with such dignity, before the decadence of eyesight painting made artists lose their innocent idea of truth. . . ." Carpaccio, Mantegna, Giovanni Bellini and Piero della Francesca became principal sources of inspiration, replacing Renoir and Delacroix, if not Rembrandt, in his pantheon.

In such paintings as *Santa Fe Siesta, Monument on the Plaza, Tea for One,* and *Model with Red Hand Mirror* (nos. 170, 172, 173 and 175), Sloan creates fullness of

JOHN SLOAN: HIS GRAPHICS

E. John Bullard

FROM EARLY CHILDHOOD ON John Sloan was exposed to the best English and American graphic art. His great-uncle, Alexander Priestley, had a large library which included folios of Hogarth and Rowlandson prints, and books illustrated by Cruikshank and Doré. As a child, Sloan also saw the illustrations of Keene, du Maurier, and Leech, in such English periodicals as *Punch,* and the work of the leading American illustrators in *Harper's Monthly.* Sloan's maternal aunt had married an Englishman, William H. Ward, son of the founder of Marcus Ward and Co., a leading publisher and manufacturer of fine stationery. Sloan's father was, for a time, a traveling salesman in America for the Ward company and brought home samples of illustrated books and greeting cards designed by Kate Greenaway and Walter Crane for his children. This early exposure to fine illustration was an important element in the development of Sloan's own graphic style.[1]

In 1888 Sloan left school to take a position as an assistant cashier with Porter and Coates, then Philadelphia's leading bookseller and print dealer. Sloan made pen and ink copies of Rembrandt and Dürer prints in the store's inventory and did his first etchings at this time.

In 1890 Sloan joined A. Edward Newton's fancy goods business as a decorator and designer of novelties and illustrator of small gift publications. The following year, he became a free-lance artist, continuing to work on commission for Newton and others. His most important account was the Bradley Coal Company of Philadelphia. Once a month he would design a streetcar poster for this firm, with accompanying doggerel praising the company's product. This work continued for more than ten years, resulting in over 120 posters of which, unfortunately, only six have survived.[2]

In 1892, Sloan joined the staff of the Philadelphia *Inquirer.* Lacking the graphic agility of such artist-reporters as his friends William Glackens and George Luks, Sloan did decorative work and illustrations for the paper's feature pages and Sunday supplement. This work allowed Sloan to develop an individual graphic style.

From the beginning, Sloan's work for the *Inquirer* displayed elements of poster style design, a graphic manifestation of art nouveau. His first *Inquirer* illustration, *On the Court at Wissahickon Heights* published February 12, 1892 (nos. 3-4), showed the basic characteristics of the poster style: large areas of single tone or texture, unmodeled forms, strong, continuous contour lines, and a lack of spatial depth, emphasizing the two dimensional design.

This stylistic development was first of all due to Sloan's realization of the artistic possibilities of the line cut, a photo-mechanical process for the reproduction of black and white drawings. It was in the process's limitations that Sloan found new creative possibilities. Line cut is most effective when the contrast between black and white is emphasized. A simple use of line combined with unmodeled forms, creating solid areas of black and white, best achieves this effect.

Sloan found inspiration for his new style from several sources. Of crucial importance was the influence of Japanese art in the form of wood-block prints, known as *ukiyo-e.* By the beginning of the nineties Sloan had begun to collect Japanese prints, then available in Philadelphia. Sloan went beyond a mere superficial interest in these works. This was partly due to his admiration for Whistler's work and his understanding of that artist's oriental borrowings. Of great importance for Sloan's understanding and assimilation of Japanese art was his meeting in 1893 with Beisen Kubota, a Japanese illustrator then in America to cover the Chicago Exposition for a Tokyo newspaper.[3] Kubota taught Sloan and Robert Henri the *sumie* brush technique, with its emphasis on the contrast of black and white. Sloan became enthusiastic, carrying brush, ink, and sketchbook around so that he could practice at every opportunity.

From childhood, Sloan had known and admired the work of the English illustrator Walter Crane. From Crane, Sloan adapted the typical Pre-Raphaelite female type, that elegantly attenuated, languid figure, with heavy lidded eyes, sensual mouth, profusion of hair, and flowing draperies. This fin de siècle ideal was frequently depicted by Sloan, as in his cover design for the second volume of *Moods* (no. 11).

The poster movement really began in France in 1866 when Jules Cheret issued his first poster in Paris.[4] Cheret's strong, bold designs were marked by a graphic simplicity which eliminated details and complex modeling, relying on two dimensional space, bright colors, and large, easily read forms and letters.

A slightly later designer working in Paris was the Swiss born Eugène Grasset, whose first poster appeared in 1885. In 1889, *Harper's Monthly* commissioned Grasset to design a poster to advertise the Christmas issue,[5] an assignment followed by others during the next few years. Grasset's work had an undeniable influence on the development of American poster art in the nineties.

The "poster craze" reached its height in Europe and

America between 1895 and 1898, with distinctive and talented artists working in many countries. The poster style in America was closely associated with the proliferation of self-consciously artistic and short-lived little magazines, such as *The Chap Book* and *The Echo,* based on such English models as Aubrey Beardsley's *The Yellow Book.* They published articles, stories, and poems by local literati, usually illustrated with poster style drawings.[6] At the time, Bradley and Edward Penfield, art editor of *Harper's Monthly,* were considered America's leading poster artists.[7]

Although Sloan evolved his poster style from the same sources as his contemporaries, the question remains as to the influence of other poster artists on his development. The basic characteristics of his style were already established in his first work for the *Inquirer* in early 1892. At this date he could not have seen the work of Bradley, Penfield or Beardsley. Sloan was probably familiar with Grasset's early designs for *Harper's,* considering that magazine's large circulation and importance. In fact, of all the other poster artists, Sloan is closest to Grasset, particularly in the flattening of the design and the use of strong outlines to define and isolate forms. After 1893 Sloan surely saw the work of the other poster artists and their examples may have helped to refine his own style.

While Sloan was not the first to work in a poster style, he was probably the first, perhaps the only, artist to adapt the style to daily newspaper illustrations. Besides the newspapers, his work also appeared in many of the little magazines. He served as art editor for one in Philadelphia, called *Moods,* during its brief existence in 1895. His design for the cover and poster of the February 15, 1896, issue of *The Echo* shows his distinctive poster style at its best (no. 10-11). He had an interesting sense of patterning, using areas of texture in contrast to solid black and white. Sloan also employed a characteristic double contour line, creating a thin thread of white to separate areas of pattern and tone. In contrast to Bradley or Beardsley, Sloan's designs were never reduced to near abstract patterns. His work, especially for the newspapers, was based on memory of life observed.

In 1895 Sloan left the *Inquirer,* joining the staff of the Philadelphia *Press,* his first illustrations appearing December 15. There he did the same kind of work, in the same decorative manner. He enjoyed working for the newspapers, particularly the *Press.* Remembering those days, he later wrote:

It is not hard to recall the *Press* "art department": a dusty room with windows on Chestnut and Seventh Street—walls plastered with caricatures of our friends and ourselves, a worn board floor, old chairs and tables close together, "no smoking" signs and a heavy odor of tobacco, and Democrats (as the roaches were called in this Republican stronghold) crawling everywhere. But we were as happy a group as could be found and the fun we had took the place of college for me.[8]

In the summer of 1898, Sloan left the *Press* for the New York *Herald* where he continued to work in his poster style but resented the editorial control and interference which, in his words, "wanted drawings that were 'tickled up'." The experience was beneficial in that he learned how to use the Benday process, a photoengraving method then being newly employed for color illustration in newspapers.

In the late fall, Sloan gladly returned to Philadelphia and the *Press,* lured by their purchase of color presses and a guarantee of more space. For the next four years he was the *Press's* leading artist. Beginning in 1899 he designed a series of Sunday supplement cover pages, often printed in bright colors. As with the line cut, Sloan was interested in creatively exploiting the limitations of the mechanical process. Working with the printers, he experimented with Benday to achieve fresh and imaginative results. The best of these were full page picture puzzles, such as the *Football Puzzle* (no. 18). In these puzzles, which incorporated hidden images or had parts which required cutting or folding, Sloan's poster style reached its richest development. His designs became more complex and detailed, the line work more florid and sinuous. This late work seems closer to that of such art nouveau artists as Alfons Mucha than that of the earlier, more severe Grasset. Sloan did nearly eighty of these picture puzzles, all popular with *Press* readers, especially since cash prizes were given for their solution.

DURING THE PERIOD 1892 to 1903, most of Sloan's newspaper illustrations were done in his poster style. At the same time, he was also working in a realist manner. It was this style, developed concurrently with his poster work, which characterized Sloan's graphic production after 1903.

Familiarity with the English realist illustrators of *Punch,* particularly John Leech and Charles Keene, was crucial to the evolution of Sloan's realist style. Of the French illustrators, Sloan admired the work of Forain and Steinlen, whose drawings he saw in *Le Rire.* Regarding the latter artist, he wrote, "I like the humanism with which he drew people, and learned from him technical devices about using crayon to make 'shading' which could be used for line cut reproduction." [9] This Steinlen influence can be seen in the long, diagonal hatching of Sloan's drawing for the American *Gil Blas* (no. 12).

The humanism which Sloan found in Steinlen's drawings of Paris low life also attracted him to the graphic work of Daumier and Goya, whose choice and treatment of subject matter was important for his development. [10] As with the English illustrators, Sloan collected examples of these men's work.

By 1903 Sloan had arrived at a mature realist style. This can be seen in his illustrations for John Kendrick Bangs' weekly serial, "The Genial Idiot," which appeared in the *Press* that year (nos. 26 and 27). These drawings, not finished in an academic sense, are sketchy and open. The diagonal crosshatching, derived from Steinlen, has been refined and sparingly used. Each character is individualized in feature and gesture, a quality of Sloan's best illustrations.

In December 1903, the Philadelphia *Press* discontinued publishing its own Sunday supplement, subscribing instead to a syndicated one. This left Sloan without a regular job. The situation was partially relieved by the *Press's* decision to continue his series of small weekly puzzles, known as "word charades," which he had recently begun. Each charade, such as "What Names for Books of Reference are Pictured Here?," featured ten panels which pictorially represented a word in that particular category. These pictorial puns were similar to those often used in his full-page picture puzzles and in his short-lived comic strip, "Paul Palette, the Practical Paintist", which appeared in 1902 (nos. 28 and 29). The charades continued after he moved to New York, finally ending in December 1910. Like the picture puzzles, they demonstrated Sloan's great imagination, both literal and visual.

IN APRIL 1904 Sloan moved to New York City, encouraged by Glackens and Everett Shinn that he would find steady employment there as a magazine illustrator. By then New York was the most important publishing center in the country. To be a successful free-lance magazine illustrator, it was vital for an artist to be close to the art departments and editors of major publications. For the next twelve years Sloan was completely dependent on his work as an illustrator, except for rare teaching assignments. But as a magazine illustrator he never experienced as great a commercial success as either Glackens or Shinn. During the period 1904 to 1907, Sloan illustrated twenty-one stories for national magazines, while for the same period Glackens

illustrated sixty-three. It was not until 1908 that Sloan began to receive magazine assignments regularly.

While Sloan did less magazine work, he illustrated more books than Glackens and Shinn—a total of forty-five between 1891 and 1938 (see page 210). Sloan's most important book assignment began in 1902 just before he moved to New York and provided him with a small, steady income for three years. This was the publication by the Frederick J. Quinby Company of the works of the mid-nineteenth century French novelist Charles Paul de Kock. [11] This Boston publisher first approached Glackens to do the illustrations, who, realizing the extent of the project, recruited his friends as additional illustrators. This group included, among others, Shinn, Luks, James Preston, and Frederick Gruger. Anticipating large sales, the Quinby Company planned to issue the de Kock novels in twelve different editions, from deluxe to popular, on a subscription basis. Each volume was to be illustrated with photogravure reproductions of drawings and original etchings. Of the fifty volumes planned, forty-two were published. Although Glackens was the first artist commissioned, Sloan executed the largest number of illustrations. This was possibly due to Glackens' dislike of the etching process, a medium which Sloan had been familiar with for ten years. In fact, the de Kock commission was his first artistically significant work in this field and the experience led him to begin his important set of New York City Life etchings in 1905. Sloan's de Kock illustrations appeared in eighteen volumes, numbering fifty-three etchings and fifty-four reproductions.

Sloan's admiration for the illustrators of *Punch* is particularly evident in the de Kock illustrations (nos. 30-32). Since artists such as Leech and Tenniel were working at the same time that de Kock was writing, Sloan turned to these English illustrators for ideas on styles of dress and fashion current in the mid-nineteenth century. Sloan, who unlike his friends had never been to Europe, was forced to use old engravings and maps of Paris and travel guides to gain a visual knowledge of the stories' settings. He succeeded marvelously, for his de Kock illustrations have a vitality and verve which quite outdistance their literary source in inventiveness and quality.

When Sloan received a magazine assignment, he first carefully read the story to decide which scenes would lend themselves best to pictorialization. Although he was often discouraged by the poor quality of the writing he was assigned to illustrate, he put a great deal of effort into his drawings. If the setting was New York, he would sketch the specific locale. Or he would go to the library to research the subject.

Most illustrators, while doing work for a variety of magazines, were usually favored by one particular publication. *Collier's Weekly* used Sloan more often than did other magazines, and between 1908 and 1913, Sloan illustrated thirty stories for this publication. This close association was due largely to Sloan's friendship with Will Bradley, the poster style artist of the nineties who served as art editor of *Collier's* between 1907 and 1910.[12] Bradley was responsible for choosing Sloan to illustrate a series of comic short stories about pirates by Ralph Bergengren. At Bradley's suggestion, Sloan adopted a special style for these drawings which simulated the appearance of the wood engravings of Thomas Bewick. These were executed on scratch board—a sheet of cardboard with a layer of compressed, white chalk as the drawing surface. Sloan would work out his design on tracing paper (no. 130), transfer it to the scratch board, redraw it freely with brush and ink, and with a knife then scratch away some of the ink on the surface to achieve crisp, sharp edges (no. 131). The final result had the appearance of an early nineteenth century wood engraving. Altogether Sloan illustrated fourteen Bergengren pirate stories in this style between 1908 and 1913. His woodcut manner proved popular and Sloan used it for other assignments, the last in 1949 when he illustrated a complete issue of the *New Mexico Quarterly*.

THE PERIOD BETWEEN 1900 and the First World War witnessed long needed social and economic reform in America. The public, awakened by muckracking writers and publications such as *McClure's Magazine,* demanded correction of the abuses and excesses of the trusts and monopolies which stifled free competition and personal initiative. Although he was not a politically oriented person, John Sloan took an active role in this Progressive movement. He was a genuine humanitarian, uninterested in doctrinaire questions of political and social philosophy.

Beginning in December 1908, Sloan became interested in the Socialist Party, then one of the most advanced and viable progressive organizations. As his commitment to the Socialist Party grew, he began to contribute drawings to such Socialist publications as *The Call* and *Progressive Woman*, always without payment. These contributions were usually cartoons satirizing contemporary events or persons (no. 82).

During the decade preceding World War I, a new group of little magazines appeared, mainly dedicated to social reform. The outstanding publication of this group was *The Masses*, founded in January 1911. Originally organized to support the Cooperative movement, a Socialist plan for consumer owned stores, it was soon publishing "socially conscious, anti-capitalist literary and artistic expressions." [13] In the fall of 1912 the magazine was reorganized by the staff into a cooperative enterprise, owned and operated by the artists and writers. Max Eastman, a former assistant in philosophy at Columbia, was selected as the new editor.

Sloan joined the staff of *The Masses* in December 1912. From the beginning of Eastman's editorship, Sloan served as art editor, although he was not credited with that title on the masthead until December 1914. Sloan and Eastman wanted to model the magazine on such humorous, political publications as the German *Simplicissimus*, with its high quality of literary and artistic contributions and its sense of satirical detachment.[14] During the period Sloan was art editor, circulation averaged about 12,000 copies an issue. Because it did not follow a strict Socialist Party line, its readership was broader than that of similar publications.

As art editor, Sloan completely redesigned *The Masses'* visual appearance, beginning with the January 1913 issue. His layout was characterized by several new ideas. First, line cut was used to reproduce the illustrations, instead of half-tone. Line cut gave clean, bright areas of white and strong blacks, in contrast to the greys of half-tone. Secondly, the illustrations were reproduced in a larger size than before, half or often full page—an innovation which artists would appreciate. Usually magazine illustrations were reduced to a size in which much of the detail and sparkle of the original was lost. Thirdly, most of these illustrations were independent of any text. They existed for themselves, as individual elements in the magazine's layout, as important as the political and literary contributions. The captions were short, direct, and to the point. Fourthly, the pages, in contrast to those of other magazines, had a clean, uncluttered appearance. There were no enframements, decorative headings, or tailpieces. Only one type face was used throughout the magazine. The cover consisted of one, full page illustration with the title across the top in bold letters (nos. 84-86, 89, 92).

The artistic quality of the illustrations was high. Sloan's criterion for a drawing's publication was always its artistic merit, not its doctrinaire message. These new graphic innovations attracted many talented artists to *The Masses* even though the magazine could not afford to pay them. Drawings by Stuart Davis, George Bellows, Boardman Robinson, Maurice Becker, and Glenn Coleman were published, in addition to the cartoons of Art Young.

Sloan's clean, direct approach to graphic design was a fresh innovation for American magazines and had an immediate effect on other publications. The most obvious impact was on *Harper's Weekly,* which came under the editorship of Norman Hapgood in 1913. Sloan himself did twenty-four drawings for Hapgood (nos. 88 and 90), including two covers. The change in *Harper's* layout introduced Sloan's innovations to a much larger audience than *The Masses* and was important in popularizing his ideas among other designers. His uncluttered approach was adopted in varying degrees by other leading American publications, including *McClure's, American Magazine,* and *Cosmopolitan.*

Sloan very likely acquired some of his ideas on magazine design from his friend Will Bradley, one of America's great typographic designers, who had attempted a few years earlier to bring a similar approach to *Collier's,* but he was not nearly as successful. In fact Sloan's accomplishments probably had an effect on Bradley's later work, particularly during the 1920s when he was art and typographic supervisor of the Hearst magazines.

The drawings Sloan did for *The Masses* are among his finest graphic creations. Altogether he created sixty-three drawings for the magazine, seven of which appeared on the cover. His work for the magazine falls into three groups: genre scenes of city life, lacking any social or political message (nos. 85, 89, 93); humorous, satirical drawings concerning topical issues; and powerful visual indictments of social injustice and brutality (nos. 87, 91, 92, 94). When depicting the underprivileged, Sloan was never condescending, but treated them with sympathy and respect.

As the editorial policy of *The Masses* became more doctrinaire, Sloan became less and less involved with the magazine. After September 1914, Sloan's contributions became less frequent, with only a few of his drawings appearing in 1915 and 1916. The final break came in late April 1916 when, after an indecisive showdown between the artists and writers, Sloan resigned as art editor. Although he continued to champion liberal causes for the rest of his life, his resignation from the Socialist Party at the time he left *The Masses* ended his political activism.

After 1916 Sloan practically gave up commercial illustration. During the years after 1920, he received only an occasional magazine or book commission, the most important being sixteen etchings for a special edition of Maugham's *Of Human Bondage* in 1938. It is possible that he found it difficult to secure magazine assignments after 1916 due to his association with *The Masses* and his strong pacifist feelings. In any case, after 1916 he supported himself by teaching art, primarily at the Art Students League of New York.

The end of Sloan's career as an illustrator did not diminish his extensive graphic production. Prompted in part by the 1913 Armory Show and in part by his role as an art teacher, he began to work regularly from a model, producing from 1912 on a large number of spontaneous and direct drawings of the human figure (nos. 95-98). These depictions of the female figure were done in a wide variety of styles, showing his interest in and knowledge of the work of such contemporaries as Picasso and Archipenko and, later, certain Renaissance masters, such as Signorelli, Donatello, and Mantegna. Many of these figure drawings relate to paintings and etchings he was working on concurrently. Sloan rarely made preparatory drawings for his New York City paintings—the three studies for *The City from Greenwich Village* being rare examples (nos. 132-34). This was also true of the many oils done during his summers at Gloucester, which were done with brush and paint directly from nature without preparatory drawings. In Santa Fe he began to occasionally make drawings outdoors with the intention of creating a landscape painting from them later in his studio (nos. 136-38) Most of these were pencil sketches, in notebooks, with color notations.

Sloan's interest in printmaking, particularly etching, continued throughout his career, resulting in over 300 prints produced between 1888 and 1949. His work in this field ranks him, along with Bellows and Hopper, as one of America's great twentieth-century printmakers. The subjects which he had painted frequently before 1920—the cityscapes and genre scenes of New York—were depicted after that date mainly in his etchings (nos. 145 and 146). The prints of the twenties became more complex in design and composition and richer in technique, due to a greater variety and subtlety of line and the occasional use of aquatint. Between 1931 and 1933, Sloan etched a series of monumental female nudes which related to his oils of the same period and represented an aspect of his search for more sculptural forms (nos. 154 and 156). His late oil technique of crosshatched forms derived in part from the linear style of his etchings. Often the more successful

Detail of No. 154.

Detail of No. 160.

results of his experiments in combining line and form are found among these prints, rather than in the paintings. John Sloan continued to draw until the end of his life— the series of monumental nudes in charcoal of 1949 being among his most powerful graphic accomplishments (no. 171).

FOOTNOTES

[1] Biographical information on Sloan's early years from John Sloan, "Early Days," *The Poster Period of John Sloan* (Lock Haven, Pa., 1967); and John Sloan, "Autobiographical Notes on Etching," in Peter Morse, *John Sloan's Prints* (New Haven, 1969), pp. 382-88.

[2] Peter Morse, *John Sloan's Prints,* pp. 350-57.

[3] Y. Noguchi, "Modern Japanese Illustrators," *The Critic,* XLV, 6 (December 1904), p. 516. Kubota was working for *Kokumin Shimbun* while in America and was not, as some writers have stated, the Japanese Cultural Commissioner to the 1893 Chicago Exposition.

[4] Charles Hiatt, *Picture Posters* (London, 1895), pp. 23-30.

[5] Robert Koch, "Artistic Books, Periodicals, and Posters of the Gay Nineties," *Art Quarterly,* XXV, 4 (Winter 1962), p. 373.

[6] Ibid., pp. 374-77.

[7] Robert Koch, "Will Bradley," *Art in America,* L, 3 (1962), p. 78.

[8] John Sloan, "Artists of the Press," *Philadelphia Museum Bulletin,* XLI, 207 (November 1945), p. 7.

[9] John Sloan, "Early Days," *The Poster Period of John Sloan,* unpaged.

[10] John Sloan, *John Sloan's New York Scene* (New York, 1965), pp. 65 and 72.

[11] Information on the de Kock commission from Morse, *John Sloan's Prints,* pp. 64-67.

[12] Will Bradley, *His Chap Book* (New York, 1955), p. 94.

[13] Art Young, *Art Young: His Life and Times* (New York, 1939), p. 271.

[14] William L. O'Neill, ed., *Echoes of Revolt: The Masses 1911-1917* (Chicago, 1966), p. 17.

COLOR PLATES

GRAPHICS

Woman and Butterfly 1895

Halloween Puzzle (watercolor) 1901

Snake Charmer Puzzle 1901

PAINTINGS

The Wake of the Ferry (no. 2) 1907

South Beach Bathers 1907 and 1908

Backyards, Greenwich Village 1914

The New Blue Dress (Miss Hart) 1913

Wonson's Rocks and Ten Pound Island 1915

The City From Greenwich Village 1922

Chama Running Red 1925

Spring, Washington Square 1928 and 1950

Girl, Back to the Piano 1932

Riders in the Hills 1945

Model with Red Hand Mirror 1950

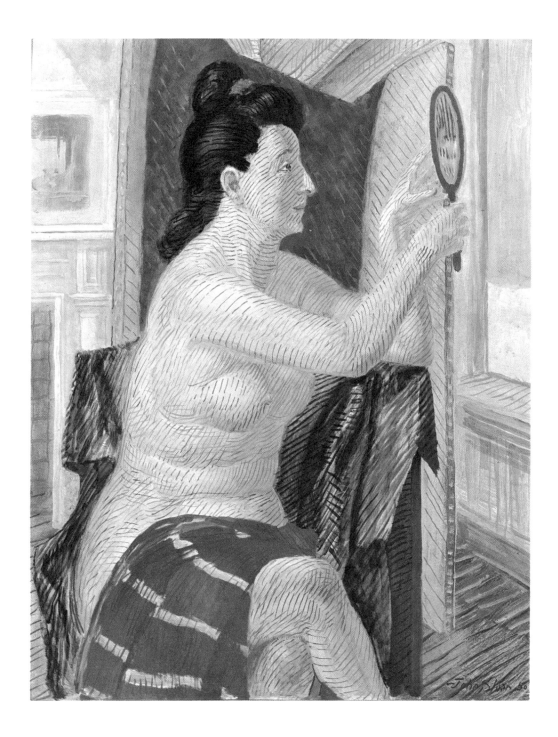

JOHN SLOAN: BIOGRAPHICAL NOTES

1871

August 2: born at Lock Haven, Pennsylvania, the son of James Dixon and Henrietta Ireland Sloan.

1876

Moved to Germantown, then to Camac Street, Philadelphia.

1884

September: entered Central High School in the same class as William Glackens and Albert C. Barnes. Enrolled in the College Preparatory Curriculum.

1888

April: left high school to go to work for Porter and Coates, booksellers and dealers in fine prints. Taught himself to etch by study of *The Etcher's Handbook* by Philip Gilbert Hamerton.

1890

Began work for A. Edward Newton, designing novelties and calendars, and making etchings. Entered night freehand drawing class at the Spring Garden Institute.

1891

Left Newton and took his own small studio as a free lance artist doing lettering, advertisements, and calendars.

1892

Began work in the art department of the Philadelphia *Inquirer*. Fall: entered Antique Class at the Pennsylvania Academy of the Fine Arts under Thomas Anshutz. Met Robert Henri.

1893

March: helped form Charcoal Club, a five months' breakaway from the Academy. Joined with Joe Laub in renting Henri's studio at 806 Walnut Street. Visit of Beisen Kubota to Philadelphia, giving lessons in Japanese brush technique.

1894

Late in '93 or early in '94, left the Academy. First public recognition as an illustrator in the poster style, from the Chicago magazines, *Inland Printer* and *Chapbook*.

1895

Art editor of *Moods: a Journal Intime*. December: left *Inquirer* for the staff of the Philadelphia *Press*.

1896

Began two murals at the Pennsylvania Academy of the Fine Arts. First serious painting in oils, chiefly portraits, 1896 and 1897.

1897

In 1897 or 1898, undertook first city scenes.

1898

Summer: went to New York to work on New York *Herald*.

October: returned to Philadelphia *Press*. Met Anna M. (Dolly) Wall.

1899

June: first large colored poster drawing for the *Press*.

1900

Illustrated Stephen Crane's *Great Battles of the World*. October: exhibited *Walnut Street Theater* at the Chicago Art Institute.
November: exhibited *Independence Square* at the Carnegie Institute, Pittsburgh.

1901

April: three paintings at Allan Gallery, New York, in group show organized by Henri.
August 5: married Anna M. Wall.

1902

By August was working on illustrations for a deluxe edition of Charles Paul de Kock's novels. (Fifty-four drawings and fifty-three etchings were completed by January, 1905).

1903

April: exhibited *Violinist, Will Bradner* at the Society of American Artists. Received critical acclaim for the de Kock etchings.
December: left Philadelphia *Press* art department but continued making "word charade" puzzles for the paper through 1910, his only regular source of income.

1904

January: exhibited with Henri group at the National Arts Club.
April: moved to New York.
September: took apartment at 165 W. 23rd Street, where he painted many of his best known city life paintings and remained seven years.

1905

Did eight of the ten etchings of the New York City Life set. Received Honorable Mention for *The Coffee Line* at the Eighth International of the Carnegie Institute.

1906

January 1: began diary (continued until 1913).
February: in group show at Pisinger's Modern Gallery.
May: of the ten New York etchings invited to the American Water Color Society Exhibition, four were returned as "too vulgar."
August: began outdoor sketching in oil.
December: received first enthusiastic review of a New York city scene painting, *Dust Storm, Fifth Avenue*.

1907

May: decision of The Eight to hold exhibition in 1908.
Fall: taught one day weekly at Pittsburgh Art Students League.

Discussion of Sloan's art in Charles H. Caffin,
The Story of American Painting.

1908
February: exhibition of The Eight at Macbeth Gallery.
Subsequent traveling exhibition.
May: experiments with lithography. Growing interest in
Socialist Party.

1909
February: article on Sloan in *The Craftsman*.
June: introduced to the Maratta color system by Henri.
July: met John Butler Yeats.

1910
January: joined Socialist Party.
April: Exhibition of Independent Artists.
June: major sale of prints to John Quinn.
November: Socialist party candidate for N.Y. State Assembly
(ran again in 1915).

1911
March: commissioned to illustrate six volumes by
Emil Gaboriau.
May: planning for MacDowell Club exhibitions.
June: moved to apartment at 155 E. 22nd St.
December: traveled to Omaha to paint portraits of
Mr. and Mrs. Gottlieb Storz.

1912
January: group exhibition at MacDowell Club. Elected
member of Association of American Painters and Sculptors.
May: took studio at 35 Sixth Avenue (where he remained
three years); began studies of the nude.
October: moved to apartment at 61 Perry Street.
December: became Acting Art Editor of *The Masses*. Dolly
became Business Manager (through May, 1913) and Treasurer.

1913
February: moved to apartment at 240 West Fourth Street.
February 17-March 15: International Exhibition of Modern
Art (Armory Show); two paintings, five etchings. Helped
hang exhibition. First sale of a painting, *Nude, Green Scarf*,
to Dr. Albert C. Barnes.

1914
Summer at Gloucester (returned every summer through 1918).
December: appeared as Art Editor on masthead of *The Masses*,
but became inactive thereafter as contributor.

1915
Received Bronze Medal for etching at San Francisco
Pan-Pacific Exposition.
October: moved to 88 Washington Place, where he remained
twelve years.

1916
January: first one man exhibition at Mrs. H. P. Whitney's
studio.
April: resigned from *The Masses* and subsequently left Socialist
Party. One-man exhibition sponsored by Dr. John Weischel's
People's Art Guild at Hudson Guild Social Center.
Summer: Gloucester, private classes.
September: began teaching at Art Students League, continuing
(with brief interruption) until 1938. Began life-long association
with Kraushaar Gallery.

1917
March: first one-man show at Kraushaar's.
April: helped hang the first exhibition of the Society of
Independent Artists at the Grand Central Palace.

1918
Became president of Society of Independent Artists
(held position for life). One of original members of Whitney
Studio Club.

1919
Trip to Santa Fe, New Mexico, with Randall Daveys.
(Returned every summer except 1933 and 1951.)
Duncan Phillips purchased *Old Clown Making Up* for the
recently incorporated Phillips Memorial Collection.

1920
Bought house in Santa Fe.

1921
Purchase of *Dust Storm, Fifth Avenue* by The Metropolitan
Museum of Art (first sale to a museum). Trip to Hopi
Snake Dance.

1922
Surgery for hernia.

1923
Sale of twenty oils to George Otis Hamlin (announced as
$20,000, actually $5,000).
Fall: visiting critic of art classes, Maryland Institute, Baltimore.

1924
April: member of jury of American section of Carnegie
International.

1925
Operation for hernia. Publication of A. E. Gallatin's *John Sloan*.

1926
Awarded Gold Medal for etching *Hell Hole*, Philadelphia
Sesqui-Centennial. Mrs. Whitney presented a complete set of
etchings to The Metropolitan Museum of Art.

1927

Moved to 53 Washington Square, his "first real studio," where he remained eight years.

1928

Adopted underpainting and glaze technique. Publicized sale of twenty paintings to Carl Hamilton falls through.

1929

Elected to National Institute of Arts and Letters. Beginning of superimposed linework over glazes. Death of Robert Henri.

1931

Received Carroll H. Beck Gold Medal for *Vagis, the Sculptor* at the Pennsylvania Academy. Elected President of Art Students League. Resigned teaching position at League. President, Exposition of Indian Tribal Arts. Surgery, Pueblo, Colorado.

1932

Resigned as President of Art Students League. Joined staff of Archipenko's École d'Art (November and December). A founder of Washington Square Outdoor Show.

1933

Elected head of the George Luks school and taught there until May, 1935. Summer in New York City. Letter to sixty museums offering paintings at half price; made one sale, *Pigeons,* to Museum of Fine Arts, Boston, in 1935.

1934

WPAP: painted *Tammany Hall* and *Fourteenth Street, Snow*.

1935

Returned to Art Students League. Moved to Hotel Chelsea, 222 W. 23rd St. (Retained studio apartment until his death.)

1936

March: exhibition of hundred etchings at Whitney Museum.

1937

February: Etching retrospective at Kraushaar's. Did sixteen prints illustrating Maugham's *Of Human Bondage*.

1938

Retrospective exhibition at Addison Gallery of American Art. Gall bladder operation. Death of William Glackens.

1939

Publication of *Gist of Art*. Treasury Department mural for Bronxville, N.Y., Post Office.

1940

Started to build "Sinagua," six miles from Santa Fe.

1941

Second operation for obstruction of gall duct, and double pneumonia. One-man exhibition at Museum of New Mexico.

1942

First prize ($500) for etching *Fifth Avenue, 1909,* in exhibition "Artists for Victory." Elected to Academy of Arts and Letters.

1943

May 4: death of Dolly (coronary). Third operation for obstruction of gall duct; successful. Convalescence in Santa Fe, fall and winter.

1944

February 5: married Helen Farr. Elected President Santa Fe Painters and Sculptors.

1945

Artists of the Philadelphia *Press* exhibition at the Philadelphia Museum of Art. Exhibition of etchings and Moody lecture at the Rennaissance Society of the University of Chicago. Operation to correct "double vision."

1946

Seventy-fifth Anniversary Exhibition, Dartmouth College.

1948

Retrospective exhibition, Kraushaar Gallery.

1949

Illustrated *New Mexico Quarterly*. President of New Mexico Alliance for the Arts.

1950

Gold Medal for painting, American Academy of Arts and Letters. Elected, American Academy of Arts and Sciences.

1951

Summer in Hanover, New Hampshire. September 7: died following operation.

1952

Retrospective Exhibition at Whitney Museum of American Art (selected before his death).

CATALOG

The listing of oils and graphics follows a chronological order, with occasional exceptions to permit groupings by medium or subject. Dimensions are given in inches, height before width. Descriptions of graphics and paintings are brief to avoid duplication of catalog raisonné compilations. Graphics entries with "Morse numbers" will be found fully described in Peter Morse, *John Sloan's Prints, A Catalogue Raisonné of the Etchings, Lithographs and Posters*. Unless otherwise indicated, the graphic works are all on paper. Catalog descriptions of all Sloan paintings are being compiled at the Delaware Art Museum by Grant Holcomb with the assistance of Helen Farr Sloan.

The comments accompanying the illustrations are drawn, in large part, from the remarks Sloan wrote for the reproductions in *Gist of Art*. Quotations not otherwise identified come from that source or from the commentaries he supplied for the catalogs of the Renaissance Society of Chicago *(Retrospective Exhibition of Etchings,* 1945) and Dartmouth College *(Seventy-fifth Anniversary Retrospective,* 1946).

1 SELF-PORTRAIT 1890

Oil on canvas, 14 x 11⅞ in.

Inscribed on back: J. F. Sloan, July 1890. Inscribed on reverse top
of stretcher: Stretcher made by my father for this painting James Dixon
Sloan, John Sloan.

Lent by the Delaware Art Museum, Wilmington, Gift of Mrs. John Sloan

Sloan painted this picture on window shade in the summer of
1890, before he had received formal art instruction. It is his
first oil but not his first surviving portrait: he made an etching
of his sister Marianna in 1888.

2 WILLIAM GLACKENS c. 1895

Oil on canvas, 20 x 16 in.

Lent by the Delaware Art Museum, Wilmington, Gift of Mrs. John Sloan

This painting, though undated, may be attributed to the small group of some half dozen oils that survive from the mid-nineties. The emphasis on flat shapes reflects Sloan's poster style. The portrait may date as early as 1895, when Glackens and Sloan were still closely associated in Philadelphia. (In June, 1895, Glackens sailed for Paris, and he visited Philadelphia only intermittently thereafter.)

3 ON THE COURT AT WISSAHICKON HEIGHTS 1892

Brush, pen and ink over pencil on board, 9¾ x 6⅝ in.

Inscribed at lower right: John / Sloan (monogram signature);
and in pencil: First Newspp.

Lent by the John Sloan Trust

4 ON THE COURT AT WISSAHICKON HEIGHTS 1892

Line cut reproduction, 6 x 4⅛ in.

Inscribed in pencil at lower right: *first* for the *Inquirer*

Lent by the John Sloan Trust

An examination of this drawing, Sloan's first poster style newspaper illustration, reveals that he originally intended to model
the foreground woman's dress with crosshatching but erased
the pencil lines when inking, thereby simplifying the dress
to the barest contour. His few earlier newspaper illustrations
had been done in a standard crosshatched newspaper style
and this drawing marked an important and original departure
for him.

A comparison between this reproduction, which appeared in
the Philadelphia Inquirer on February 12, 1892, and the
original drawing (no. 3) reveals the typical loss of contrast
between black and white and the reduction in scale.

54

5 NIGHT ON THE BOARDWALK 1894

Brush, pen and ink over pencil on board, 12⅜ x 6⅝ in.

Inscribed at lower right: John / Sloan (monogram signature)

Lent by the John Sloan Trust

6 ON THE PIER 1894

Brush, pen and ink over pencil, 12⅞ x 9⅝ in.

Inscribed at lower left: John / Sloan (monogram signature)

Lent by the John Sloan Trust

Illustration for an article on Seaside Resorts in the July 8, 1894, Inquirer. *The decorative signature on this drawing was used by Sloan until 1905, and seems most appropriate for his poster style work. A single, elongated "S" curve served as the initial letter of his first and last names, which were spelled out one above the other.*

Done for an article on Atlantic City for the resort page of the Inquirer *Sunday supplement, this drawing was published at least twice, on July 22 and August 12, 1894. It was also used in the same year to illustrate an article on Sloan's poster style in the* Inland Printer *and as one of four of his drawings to appear in the* Chap Book. *These two early notices of his work, along with another article in the* Decorator and Furnisher *in 1896, brought Sloan national recognition for his poster style work.*

7 THE COUPLE   1894

Brush, pen and ink over pencil, 10 x 6⅝ in.

Inscribed at lower right: John / Sloan (monogram signature)

Lent by Herbert S. Adler, New York

8 SAND LARKING   c. 1894

Brush, pen and ink over pencil on board, 18⅝ x 8½ in.

Inscribed at lower left: John / Sloan (monogram signature)

Lent by the John Sloan Trust

Illustration for "Sentence of Death" by H. E. Clark in the July 22, 1894, Inquirer.

Another Atlantic City illustration for the Inquirer, *which with its elongated vertical format, flat two-dimensionality, and rich use of patterns is an excellent example of the influence of Japanese prints on Sloan's poster style.*

9 WOMAN AND BUTTERFLY   1895

Chalk-plate on board, 7¼ x 5 in.

Inscribed in plate at lower left: John/Sloan (monogram signature)

Lent by the John Sloan Trust

10 POSTER FOR MOODS   1895

Chalk-plate, in green ink, 19 x 11 in.

Inscribed in pencil at lower right: John Sloan

Lent by the John Sloan Trust

(Morse H)

Cover for the second volume (dated July 25, 1895) of Moods,
A Journal Intime, *the Philadelphia little magazine for which
Sloan served as art editor. The publication lasted for only three
issues. The influence of Walter Crane and the Pre-Raphaelites
is apparent in this beautiful design.*

Poster advertising the second volume of Moods, an Illustrated
Quarterly for the Modern.

11 THE ECHO   1895

Photomechanical relief line cut, in black and red ink, 9⅞ x 5¾ in.

Lent by the John Sloan Trust

(Morse I)

12 STREET SCENE   1895

Black chalk and ink, 15¾ x 7¾ in.

Inscribed at lower left: John / Sloan (monogram signature)

Lent by the John Sloan Trust

(Morse J)

Designed as the cover of the Chicago little magazine, The Echo *(appearing on the February 15, 1896 issue), it was also used as a poster (under the mat are the words For Sale Here), which was first advertised as available to collectors in the November 1, 1895, issue. The magazine's editor, Percival Pollard, had specifically requested Sloan to design a cover for him, indicating his growing reputation in this field.*

Illustration for "Love's Kalender," a poem by P. J. Coleman, in the November 9, 1895, issue of Gil Blas, *a Philadelphia little magazine modeled after the famous French illustrated weekly of the same name.*

13 CINDER-PATH TALES   1896

Photomechanical lithograph, in black and brown ink, on brown
paper, 22¾ x 13⅞ (paper), 17¼ x 11⅛ in. (picture)

Lent by the John Sloan Trust

(Morse L)

*A poster advertising the publication of a book of short stories
by William Lindsey, published in 1896 by Copeland and Day,
Boston. This design, reduced, was also used on the book's cover.
The poster was produced by George H. Walker & Co.,
Lithographers, Boston.*

14 WHAT ARE THE WILD WAVES SAYING?　1900

Color line cut reproduction, 22⅝ x 18 in. (paper)

Lent by the John Sloan Trust

One of the nearly eighty full page puzzles Sloan did for the Philadelphia Press between 1899 and 1902, many of which, like this example, were printed in full color using the Benday process. This puzzle appeared on the cover of the Sunday supplement of July 22, 1900, and asked the readers: "What are the wild waves saying? If you examine them closely you will soon discover words hidden in the sea. Put them together in a sentence. The first correct answer received will be rewarded with the first prize of $5, and each of the next five received will win $1."

15 SNAKE CHARMER PUZZLE   1901

Color line cut reproduction, 22⅜ x 17¾ in. (paper)

Lent by the John Sloan Trust

"Here you have a snake charmer and a man who is playing the flute for her. Can you find the man? . . ." This puzzle appeared in the May 5, 1901, Press *Sunday supplement.*

16 HALLOWEEN PUZZLE   1901

Watercolor and pen and ink over pencil on board, 22⅜ x 22 in.

Inscribed at lower right: SL • • N

Lent by the John Sloan Trust

A comparison between this drawing and the Benday reproduction (no. 17) shows the unfortunate loss of color richness and crisp detail caused by the mechanical process.

17 HALLOWEEN PUZZLE   1901

Color line cut reproduction, 22⅝ x 17¾ in. (paper)

Lent by the John Sloan Trust

*"Here we have a lady giving herself a Halloween Party. She
has just thrown an apple paring over her shoulder. Its meaning
is not apparent until she finds that she can cut it into six letters
that spell the name of her future husband. Can you show how
she cut the paring? . . ." This appeared in the October 27, 1901,
Press.*

Color line cut reproduction, 22⅜ x 17¾ in. (paper)

*"Here is the Varsity Girl with ten little football players around
her. There is still another one near her who can not be seen at
first glance. Can you find the eleventh little football player? . . ."
This puzzle appeared in the October 13, 1901, Press.*

19 WALNUT STREET THEATRE (THE OLD WALNUT STREET THEATRE) c. 1899 or 1899/1900

Oil on canvas, 25 x 32 in.

Inscribed at lower right: John / Sloan (monogram signature)

Lent by the John Sloan Trust

Of all the early Philadelphia scenes, this most prefigures Sloan's developed New York work in its freedom of technique, atmosphere and relation of figures to setting. It was the first of Sloan's oils shown at a national exhibition (Chicago Art Institute, October, 1900).

20 INDEPENDENCE SQUARE, PHILADELPHIA   1900

Oil on canvas, 27 x 22 in.

Inscribed at lower right: John / Sloan (monogram signature)

Lent by the John Sloan Trust

Sloan chose this painting to represent his work in several early exhibitions, including the Carnegie International (Pittsburgh) in November, 1900 and the Society of American Artists (New York City) in April of 1901.

21 EAST ENTRANCE, CITY HALL, PHILADELPHIA   1901

Oil on canvas, 27 x 36 in.

Inscribed at upper right: John / Sloan (monogram signature)

Lent by The Columbus Gallery of Fine Arts, Columbus, Ohio, The Howald Fund

"In the late 90s a load of hay, a hansom cab, and a Quaker lady were no rare sight in the streets of Philadelphia." The most monumental composition of the early Philadelphia paintings, and one of the first in which the street actors come into independent life.

22 THE RATHSKELLER, PHILADELPHIA   1901

Oil on canvas, 35½ x 27¼ in.

Inscribed at lower right: John/Sloan (monogram signature)

Lent by The Cleveland Museum of Art, Gift of Hanna Fund

The arabesque of the woman's silhouette still recalls the poster style. The motif: "the divided attention in the young lady with a beer escort whose lonely neighbor is buying champagne." The first of Sloan's oils to develop the sort of human comedy motif that was to characterize his best-known New York scenes.

23 VIOLINIST, WILL BRADNER   1903

Oil on canvas, 37 x 37 in.

Inscribed at lower right: John/Sloan 1903 (monogram signature)

Lent by the Delaware Art Museum, Wilmington, Gift of Mrs. John Sloan

*Sloan's early portraits move step by step toward stronger and
surer modeling, the beginning of a life-long concern with
sculptural form.*

24 STEIN, PROFILE (FOREIGN GIRL)   1905

Oil on canvas, 36 x 27 in.

Inscribed at lower right: John Sloan '05

Lent by the John Sloan Trust

This sturdy painting, one of Sloan's first after moving to New York, forms a revealing contrast to Henri's more elegant version of the same model, Young Woman in White *(1904), in the National Gallery of Art (Washington). "Stein (Zenka) called and we enjoyed her visit as usual. She's a great girl, so ingenuous, so paintable, the best professional model in New York probably. . . ." (Diary, January 18, 1908). See also no. 117.*

25 THE COFFEE LINE   1905

Oil on canvas, 21½ x 31½ in.

Inscribed at lower right: John/Sloan 1905 (monogram signature)

Lent by the John Sloan Trust

*"Winter night, Fifth Avenue at Madison Square, and a long
line of cold and hungry men waiting their turn for a cup of
coffee. This gratuity was a kindly gesture on the part of one of
the newspapers."* The overtone of social concern is stronger
than usual in Sloan's painting, but this picture attracted favor-
able comment and won an Honorable Mention at the Carnegie
Institute in 1905.

26 THE GENIAL IDIOT: THE HUNGRY CAT   1903

Crayon and pencil, 18½ x 22 in.

Inscribed at lower right: J. Sloan

27 THE GENIAL IDIOT: AT THE BREAKFAST
TABLE   1903

Crayon and pencil, 18 x 16⅝ in.

Inscribed at lower left: SL • • N

*One of a series of drawings, usually reproduced
half page, which illustrated the humorous
stories of John Kendrick Bangs, which appeared
weekly in the* Press *during 1903. These stories
about the advice given on various subjects by a
bachelor at a boarding house table were quite
popular. These drawings are among his most
ambitious and successful realist newspaper
illustrations.*

*Another illustration for a John Kendrick Bangs story which
appeared in the* Press *in 1903. The two men at the right top
edge are Robert Henri and Sloan, while the woman serving
them is the artist's wife, Dolly. Sloan often included portraits
or caricatures of himself and friends in his illustrations.*

28 "JUST LEAVE ME OUT THIS TIME" 1903

Line cut reproduction, in brown ink, 10⅝ x 16⅛ in. (paper)

Lent by the John Sloan Trust

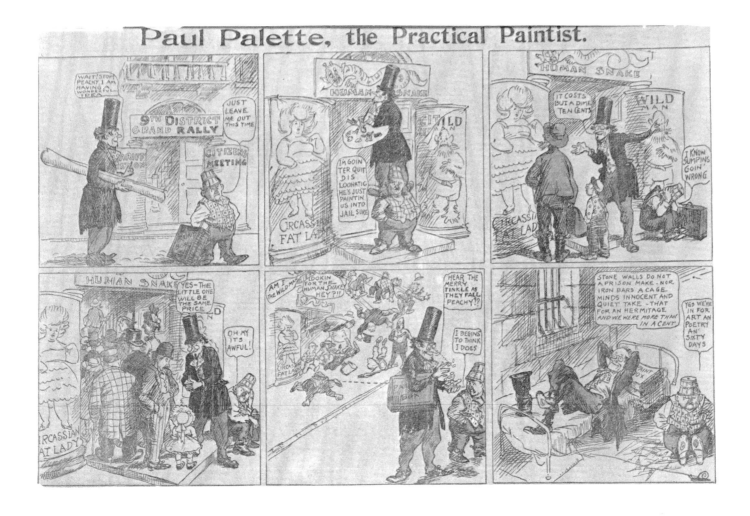

*An episode from Sloan's short-lived comic strip, "Paul Palette,
the Practical Paintist," which appeared in the* Press *in 1903.
The face of Paul Palette is a caricature of Sloan's own features.*

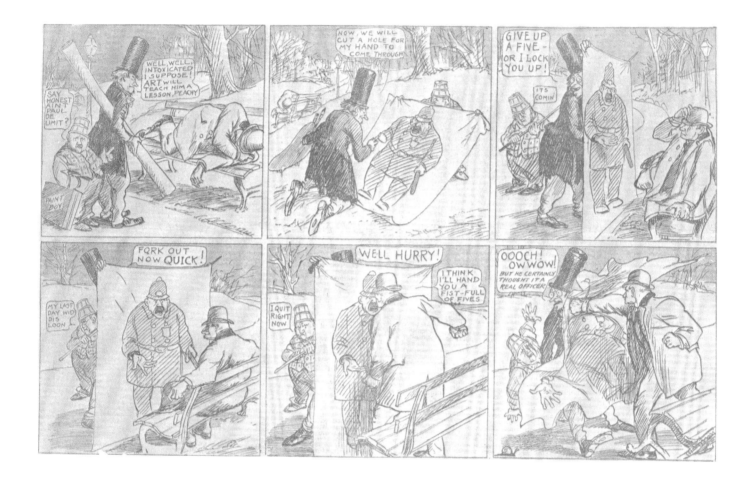

Another adventure of "Paul Palette, the Practical Paintist."

30 HE WAS QUICKLY PLACED IN HIS CARRIAGE   1904

Wash and charcoal on board, 10¼ x 14 in.

Inscribed at lower right: 1904 John/Sloan (monogram signature)

Lent by the John Sloan Trust

A drawing for volume 2 of Charles Paul de Kock's André the
Savoyard, *published in 1904, illustrating:*

. . . I drew the trigger, wretch that I was. The marquis was
stretched on the ground. I ran towards him, he was bleeding
profusely from a wound he had received in the right side. "It is
nothing," said he, "call my carriage, help me into it, the sooner
I reach the hotel the better for me."

31 MADAME FLAMBART LEFT HER HANDS IN THE
MORTAR   1904

Wash and charcoal, with touches of white, on board, 11¾ x 7⅛ in.

Inscribed at lower left: John/Sloan/04 (monogram signature)

Lent by the John Sloan Trust

An illustration for the following scene in de Kock's Madame
Pantalon, *published in 1904:*

"Plaster whitens the skin," she said. "I am not sorry to have an
occasion for trying it, it will take away the freckles I have on
my hands; I shall put both of them into it." And Madame
Flambart left both her hands in the mortar and forgot to stir it.
But the cement, which had received very little water, suddenly
became stiff. . . .

32 KISSING THE LADIES 1904

Charcoal, with touches of white, 14 x 9⅝ in.

Inscribed at lower left: John/Sloan 04 (monogram signature)

Lent by the John Sloan Trust

An illustration for the following scene in volume 2 of de Kock's
Cherami, *published in 1905:*

She tendered her cheeks to him, saying, "Kiss me and I will
forgive your disappearance from Passy." Cherami thought the
punishment rather severe, and while this was going on, Madame Capucine profited by it to tender her cheek, saying,
"Do the same to me that I may forgive you also."

33 "HE CLUTCHED THE BIG FELLOW'S HAT"   1904

Crayon with pen and ink, 10½ x 15¼ in. (mat opening)

Inscribed at lower right: John/Sloan 04 (monogram signature)

Lent by the John Sloan Trust

This drawing illustrates the following passage from Harvey J. O'Higgins' short story, "The Steady," which appeared in the August 1905 McClure's Magazine:

The next time they met—some days later, in the train—he rose at once to give her his seat, and she refused it; and while he was blushing and protesting that he would rather stand, a heavy laborer shoved past him and sat down. . . . "Get up," he said huskily. "That's her seat." The man grunted and sat back to read. Then, with a little frightened gulp, he clutched the big fellow's hat and jumped back with it to the open door.

34 "AIN'T IT BETTER THAN CHOC'LATE?"   1904

Crayon with pen and ink, 13½ x 20⅝ in. (mat opening)

Inscribed at lower right: John/Sloan/04 (monogram signature)

Lent by the John Sloan Trust

Another of the five illustrations which Sloan did for Harvey J. O'Higgins' "The Steady" (no. 33), this one set in Central Park:

They . . . took an empty table facing the splash of the fountain and the breeze from the lake. They ordered two dishes of "strawberry"; and it seemed to him that it was the first he had ever eaten ice-cream. "Ain't it better than choc'late?" she asked him.

35 PIDDLIN' ROUN'   1904

Crayon and pen and ink, 15¾ x 9½ in.

Inscribed at upper left: John/Sloan/04 (monogram signature)

Lent by the John Sloan Trust

A proposed page layout, with two illustrations, for a poem by the black writer, Paul Laurence Dunbar. This drawing was rejected by Henry Fangel, the art editor of Good Housekeeping, who wrote Sloan, "I won't exactly say that your drawings caricature the negro, but if you could present the subject in a more pleasant, attractive way (attractive to the average taste, of course) that would meet the proposition better . . . and . . . I would just as soon sacrifice the culinary and other utensils introduced down the sides of the page." It is not known whether or not Sloan submitted another version.

36 CONNOISSEURS OF PRINTS   1905

Etching, 5 x 7 in. (plate)

Inscribed in pencil at lower right: John Sloan

Lent by the John Sloan Trust

(Morse 127)

*In 1905 Sloan began a series of etchings of New York subjects,
similar to those he was then beginning to paint. Known as the*
New York City Life *set, there were originally ten etchings (nos.
36-45) in the group. Some years later, he added three more
prints to the set, executed in the same format. The set in this
exhibition are all artist's proofs, which Sloan sold to the famous
collector John Quinn in 1910, and later bought back from his
estate. This etching, the first of the set, depicts "an exhibition
of prints that were to be auctioned at the old American Art
Galleries on 23rd Street. The first of a series of 'Connoisseurs'
planned but never made."*

37 FIFTH AVENUE CRITICS   1905

Etching, 5 x 7 in. (plate)

Inscribed in pencil at lower right: John Sloan

Lent by the John Sloan Trust

(Morse 128)

"These were typical of the fashionable ladies who used to drive up and down the Avenue about four o'clock of an afternoon, showing themselves and criticizing other." The New York City Life *etchings have much of the humor and penetrating observation of life that is found in the lithographs of the French bourgeoisie by Daumier, an artist Sloan greatly admired.*

38 THE SHOW CASE 1905

Etching, 5 x 7 in. (plate)

Inscribed in pencil at lower right: John Sloan

Lent by the John Sloan Trust

(Morse 129)

*"Material from West 23rd Street and Sixth Avenue appealed
to me at this time. The devices of the toilette, which were then
secrets, created more excitement among the adolescents than
they would today," the artist wrote in 1945.*

39 MAN MONKEY 1905

Etching, 5 x 7 in. (plate)

Inscribed in pencil at lower right: John Sloan

Lent by the John Sloan Trust

(Morse 130)

*"In the side streets of the Chelsea and Greenwich Village
districts, the one man band with hand organ accompanist
furnished free entertainment to those who dropped no pennies.
He worried the horse-drawn traffic of the time, but before many
years the automobile and motor truck cleared him from the
streets."*

40 FUN, ONE CENT   1905

Etching, 5 x 7 in. (plate)

Inscribed in pencil at lower right: John Sloan 1905

Lent by the John Sloan Trust

(Morse 131)

"The Nickelodeon, with its hand-cranked moving photographs, was one of the attractions preceding the moving picture theatres (see no. 57). The one in which I garnered this bouquet of laughing girls was for many years on 14th Street near Third Avenue." This impression, the artist's proof, is inscribed, under the mat, "23rd Street near 7th Avenue."

41 THE WOMAN'S PAGE   1905

Etching, 5 x 7 in. (plate)

Inscribed in pencil at lower right: John Sloan 1905

Lent by the John Sloan Trust

(Morse 132)

On television, in 1949, Sloan said of this print, "The psychologists say we all have a little peeper instinct, and that's a result of peeping—the life across from me when I had a studio on 23rd Street. This woman in this sordid room, sordidly dressed—undressed—with a poor kid crawling around on a bed—reading the Women's Page, getting hints on fashion and housekeeping. That's all. It's the irony of that I was putting over."

42 TURNING OUT THE LIGHT   1905

Etching, 5 x 7 in. (plate)

Inscribed in pencil at lower right: John Sloan/1905

Lent by the John Sloan Trust

(Morse 134)

In 1906 Sloan was invited by a member of the committee on etchings of the American Water Color Society to send his New York City Life *set to the Society's May exhibition. Four of the prints, including this one, were returned to him as being too vulgar to exhibit. Sloan was furious and demanded that the set be returned immediately, but the acceptable six were exhibited anyway.*

43 MAN, WIFE, AND CHILD   1905

Etching, 5 x 7 in. (plate)

Inscribed in pencil at lower right: John Sloan

Lent by the John Sloan Trust

(Morse 135)

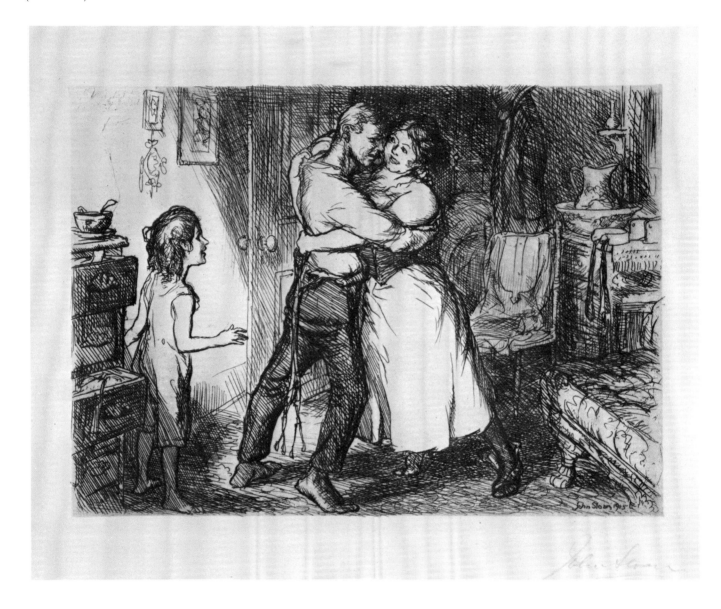

44 ROOFS, SUMMER NIGHT   1906

Etching, 5¼ x 7 in. (plate)

Inscribed in pencil at lower right: John Sloan 1906

Lent by the John Sloan Trust

(Morse 137)

*"I have always liked to watch the people in the summer,
especially the way they live on the roofs."*

89

45 THE LITTLE BRIDE   1906

Etching, 5¼ x 7 in. (plate)

Inscribed in pencil at lower right: John Sloan

Lent by the John Sloan Trust

(Morse 138)

"Back in 1906 there was a considerable French population north of 23rd Street, and the church near Proctor's Theatre was known as the French Church. The stone steps down which these newlyweds are escaping have since been removed." Inscribed on this proof of the tenth etching in the New York City Life *set, under the mat, is "St. Vincent de Paul Church 23rd Street."*

46 THE PICNIC GROUNDS   1906 and 1907

Oil on canvas, 24 x 36 in.

Inscribed at lower right: John Sloan

Lent by the Whitney Museum of American Art, New York

*"Woods near Bayonne, New Jersey, are the scene in which
these adolescent boys and girls frolic like bear cubs." Sloan may
well have been influenced by Glackens' park scenes, but his
vision was quite different. He recounts his visit to Bayonne and
his start on the painting (from memory, as was his custom) in
the Diary for May 30 and June 2, 1906.*

47 DUST STORM, FIFTH AVENUE   1906

Oil on canvas, 22 x 27 in.

Inscribed at lower right: John Sloan 1906

Lent by The Metropolitan Museum of Art, New York, George A. Hearn Fund, 1921

"In the afternoon, walking on Fifth Avenue, we were on the edge of a beautiful wind storm, the air full of dust and a sort of panicky terror in all the living things in sight. A broad gray curtain of cloud pushing over the zenith, the streets in wicked dusty murk" (Diary, 10 June 1906). This painting, which may be considered the first fully typical New York "Sloan," won him his first high acclaim from a critic when it was exhibited at the National Academy of Design in December, 1906.

48 THE COT   1907

Oil on canvas, 36¼ x 30 in.

Inscribed at lower left: John Sloan — 1907

Lent by the Bowdoin College Museum of Art, Brunswick, Hamlin Collection

"Like all pictures of this period, an extremely limited palette, providing many variants in the whites and grays. The canvas is permeated with a sense of great peace emanating from a personality." It was included in The Eight exhibition and provoked attacks which led Sloan to comment later, *"How strange to know that this type of picture was regarded as the work of a 'revolutionist in art' by the art criticism of the period in which it was painted."*

49 EASTER EVE   1907

Oil on canvas, 32 x 26 in.

Inscribed at lower left: John Sloan '07

Lent by Miss Ruth Martin, New York

*"The subject has been felt as well as seen, and is rendered with
a vigorous generalization that selects for emphasis just what is
needed to impress the spectator with the effect produced on
the artist's own mind." (Caption for* Easter Eve *in* The Story
of American Painting *by Charles H. Caffin, 1907). Included
in* The Eight *exhibition.*

50 THE WAKE OF THE FERRY (no. 2)   1907

Oil on canvas, 26 x 32 in.

Inscribed at lower left: John Sloan

Lent by The Phillips Collection, Washington

*Sloan recalled that the theme was "perhaps evoked by some
nostalgic yearning for Philadelphia. The ferry of course is the
first lap of the road home." This painting was featured on the
John Sloan commemorative stamp, issued in Lock Haven,
Pennsylvania, August 2, 1971.*

*Sloan's diary records the ride that inspired the first version
of this subject (March 19, 1907) and his later damaging the
painting (April 5). A month later he began to paint a second
version, a rarity in his work. Subsequently he had the first
picture repaired; it is now at The Detroit Institute of Arts.*

95

51 NURSEMAIDS, MADISON SQUARE   1907

Oil on canvas, 24 x 32 in.

Inscribed at lower right: John Sloan

Lent by the University of Nebraska, Lincoln, The F. M. Hall Collection

"A group of young hoydens on an early spring day are very
consciously entertaining the men of leisure who occupy the
benches. Meanwhile their young charges shift for themselves.
Paintings of this period show my resistance of the impressionist
influences." The painting dates from April, 1907, and was
included in The Eight exhibition.

52 MRS. HENRY REUTERDAHL   1907

Oil on canvas, 32 x 26 in.

Inscribed at lower left: John Sloan

Lent by Mr. and Mrs. Philip Berman, Allentown

The painting shows the effect of spontaneous attack, so prized
by Henri, but Sloan's diary records that he painted the sitter
again and again during the month of May, 1907, trying to get
"a thing that will last."

53 HAIRDRESSER'S WINDOW   1907

Oil on canvas, 31⅞ x 26 in.

Inscribed at lower left: John Sloan 07

Lent by the Wadsworth Atheneum, Hartford,
The Ella Gallup Sumner and Mary Catlin Sumner Collection

*"Walked up to Henri's studio. On the way saw a humorous
sight of interest. A window, low, second story, bleached blond
hairdresser bleaching the hair of a client. A small interested
crowd about."* Sloan noted the scene in his Diary on June 5, and
the next day he returned for a second look before starting to
paint.

   Pictures such as this brought Sloan fame as the "American
Hogarth" but so identified him with satire that for years certain
critics failed to perceive his broader intent as an artist.

54 SIXTH AVENUE AND THIRTIETH STREET   1907

Oil on canvas, 26 x 32 in.

Inscribed at lower left: John Sloan 1907

Lent by Mr. and Mrs. Meyer P. Potamkin, Philadelphia

*On June 12, 1907, Sloan recorded "a walk along Sixth Avenue,"
and on the next day wrote, "I painted, starting a 'gray day
Sixth Avenue,' Tenderloin section." He later commented "This
canvas has surely caught the atmosphere of the Tenderloin:
drab, shabby, happy, sad and human." He used the same title
for another Sixth Avenue subject, a lithograph of 1908 (no. 58).
This painting was included in The Eight exhibition.*

Oil on canvas, 26 x 31⅛ in.

Inscribed at lower right: John Sloan, 07

Lent by The Brooklyn Museum

"This old dance hall on Sixth Avenue, famous through infamy, was a well-known hangout for the underworld. Ladies whose dress and general deportment were satisfactory to the doorman were admitted free. Gents paid." The painting was begun on September 6 and completed within two weeks; the following March it was exhibited at the National Academy of Design.

56 ELECTION NIGHT IN HERALD SQUARE   1907

Oil on canvas, 26 x 32 in.

Inscribed at lower left: John Sloan — 1907

Lent by the Memorial Art Gallery of the University of Rochester

"... *The principal spot for the gathering of hilarious crowds
on Election Night was Herald Square, Sixth Avenue and 34th
Street.*" *Included in The Eight exhibition. Underlying the
buffoonery of this painting was Sloan's growing interest in
politics, which culminated three years later in his running for
office on the Socialist ticket.*

57 MOVIES, FIVE CENTS 1907

Oil on canvas, 23½ x 30½ in.

Inscribed at lower right: John Sloan, 07

Lent by Mr. and Mrs. Herbert A. Goldstone, New York

"At the time when this picture was painted, the cinema was in its sordid infancy, the auditorium a vacant store, admission a nickel. It is interesting to note that the theme of the painting still endures." Included in The Eight exhibition.

58 SIXTH AVENUE AND THIRTIETH STREET   1908

Lithograph, with crayon additions, 14 x 11 in. (design)

Lent by the National Gallery of Art, Washington, Rosenwald Collection

(Morse 142)

59 AMATEUR LITHOGRAPHERS   1908

Lithograph, 18½ x 15½ in. (stone)

Inscribed (in the stone) at lower right: J.S. 08

Lent by the John Sloan Trust

(Morse 144)

Of Sloan's more than 300 prints, only ten are lithographs. This was due in part to the technical problems of printing and the fact that he did not have the proper press available. As with etching. Sloan learned lithography from studying books. In his Diary for May 20, 1908, he writes, "Started a tissue drawing to put on stone. A girl of the streets starting out of 27th Street, early night, little girls looking at her." In this impression, Sloan changed and enriched the composition with crayon. By shifting the position of the woman's feet, he gave the figure a forward, striding movement.

Here Sloan, at the right, and Carl Moellmann, a friend and professional printer, struggle with one of Sloan's lithographs, on a press borrowed from Arthur G. Dove. On this impression, under the mat, the artist has written, "Amateur Lithographers/ This stone recorded my arduous efforts in / printing my first self printed stone / 'The Mother of the first King' (prehistoric mother) / John Sloan / This proof for John Quinn Esq."

60 FISHING FOR LAFAYETTES 1908

Oil on canvas, 8½ x 10½ in.

Inscribed at lower left: John Sloan

Lent by Mr. and Mrs. Arthur G. Altschul, New York

*In August of 1906 Sloan bought a sketch box and began to
paint small landscapes (9 x 11 in.) directly from nature on his
summer trips to Pennsylvania and New Jersey. On August 28,
1908, he decided to try a direct sketch in Manhattan: "In the
afternoon, I took my sketch box and, with much dread of what
might happen, I walked down to the 22nd Street pier of the
Coney Island boats and, after loitering about screwing up my
courage, I finally got to work. Sat on the stringpiece and made
a sketch of a group of men and boys fishing from a float. The
season has been a very good one for what they call 'Lafayettes,'
a small fish, of which I saw several very good 'strings.' I was,
in a moment, the center of a great crowd of boys, etc. . . . At
about 4:30 I left with a huge sense of achievement in having
made my sketch in the face of a mob's criticism."*

61 WILLIAM S. WALSH (PORTRAIT OF A MAN)   1908

Oil on canvas, 32 x 26 in.

Inscribed at lower right: John Sloan — 08

Lent anonymously

" 'Billy' Walsh was for several years literary editor of the New York Herald. *A burly man with a mind of the first order, a a fountain of information. . . . New York's bohemians loved him."*
    Sloan records that, after several sittings and false starts, he felt he had "a good thing from him" on February 25. The painting was sent off at once to the National Academy, where Sloan saw it "on the line" (March 13). But its ruggedness provoked criticism, and Mrs. Walsh "didn't think I had the finer side of his nature" (Diary, January 14, 1909).

62 SOUTH BEACH BATHERS   1907 and 1908

Oil on canvas, 26 x 32 in.

Inscribed at lower left: John Sloan — '08

Lent by the Walker Art Center, Minneapolis

"This Staten Island resort had few visitors compared to Coney Island, and gave better opportunity for observation of individual behavior." Sloan first visited South Beach on June 23, 1907, and admired the subject, which he began to paint from memory the following day. However, he put the painting aside and did not finish it until July, 1908.

63 DOLLY WITH A BLACK BOW   1909

Oil on canvas, 32 x 26 in.

Unsigned

Lent by the Whitney Museum of American Art, New York, Gift of Miss Amelia Elizabeth White

*"It has always seemed to me that one's own family are the
painter's most difficult sitters. It is perhaps because his mind is
divided between the creative and the critical." This is one of
the most relaxed and direct of Sloan's many portrayals of his
first wife, Dolly.*

64 CHINESE RESTAURANT   1909

Oil on canvas, 26 x 32 in.

Inscribed at lower left: John Sloan

Lent by the Memorial Art Gallery of the University of Rochester

*On February 23, 1909, "felt restless so went to the Chinese
restaurant and was glad I did for I saw a strikingly gotten up
girl with dashing red feathers in her hat playing with the
restaurant's fat cat." Sloan painted the picture a month later,
and it was accepted by the National Academy the following
December. Looking back at the painting he commented,
"Graphic expression and resonant color."*

65 THREE A.M.   1909

Oil on canvas, 32 x 26 in.

Inscribed at lower right: John Sloan

Lent by the Philadelphia Museum of Art, Gift of Mrs. Cyrus McCormick

"Night vigils at the back window of a Twenty-third Street studio were rewarded by motifs of this sort. . . . This picture is redolent with the atmosphere of a poor, back, gaslit room. It has beauty, I'll not deny it: it must be that human life is beautiful." In the Diary, April 28, Sloan noted, "A good day's work, painting on a subject that has been stewing in my mind for some weeks. I have been watching a curious two room house-hold, two women and, I think, two men, their day begins after midnight, they cook at 3 A.M." When the painting was rejected by the National Academy in March, 1910, Sloan commented, "sent as much as a joke like slipping a pair of men's drawers into an old maid's laundry." He exhibited it in The Independents exhibition the next month.

66 FIFTH AVENUE, NEW YORK   1909

Oil on canvas, 32 x 26 in.

Inscribed at lower left: John Sloan

Lent by Mrs. John F. Kraushaar, New York

The genesis of this painting is recorded in the Diary entry for
November 20, 1908:

. . . Went for a walk out Fifth Avenue. . . . The weather is clear
and mild, and Fifth Ave. was choked with automobiles, the
sidewalks crowded with women in expensive gowns. The present Directoire style (as they call it) is right interesting, giving
a dashing look—large hats set down on the head—and dresses
being scant in the skirts, not full as lately, show the legs as they
are gathered in one hand to hold the length from the ground.

67 BIG HAT (BLOND GIRL)   1909

Oil on canvas, 32¾ x 26¾ in.

Inscribed at lower left: John Sloan '09

Lent by the Milwaukee Art Center, the Layton Art Gallery Collection

*During 1909 Sloan painted a number of study portraits of
women, some with very fluent brushwork, others (like* Yolande
in Large Hat, *no. 68) with a more sculptured treatment. In
June of 1909 Sloan was introduced to the Maratta color system
by Henri, and his paintings of the period reflect a growing
interest in color.*

68 YOLANDE IN LARGE HAT (THE HAWK)   1909 or 1910

Oil on canvas, 26 x 32 in.

Unsigned

Lent by the John Sloan Trust

*"An elfin personality was Yolande. . . ." During 1909 and 1910
Sloan painted "several canvases devoted to the attempt to catch
and fix some of the lovely fire and spirit of this young girl. She
worked hard and liked to pose, and yet she flitted about like
a bird."*

69 PIGEONS   1910

Oil on canvas, 26 x 32 in.

Inscribed at lower right: John Sloan/1910

Lent by the Museum of Fine Arts, Boston, Charles Henry Hayden Fund

*"That canvas will carry into future time the feel and way of life
as it happened and as it was seen and understood by the artist"
(Robert Henri,* The Art Spirit, *p. 222). Sloan recorded painting
the picture in his Diary during February, 1910. On March 9 it
was returned, rejected, from the National Academy. "'Pigeons'
I rather thought had a chance to pass but I evidently under-
rated it. It rather looks as though they had cut me off from the
exhibition game: must find some way to show things." Plans for
The Independents exhibition followed and* Pigeons *was displayed in April.*

70 OLD CLOWN MAKING UP   1910

Oil on canvas, 32 x 26 in.

Inscribed at lower right: John Sloan

Lent by The Phillips Collection, Washington

A rare example of a posed genre subject. "Truth to tell this picture was painted under the inspiration of an enthusiastic model with a clown suit. One of my first results using the Maratta palette." Begun March 2, 1910, and shown at The Independents exhibition in April.

71 YEATS AT PETITPAS' 1910

Oil on canvas, 26⅜ x 32¼ in.

Inscribed at lower right: John Sloan

Lent by the Corcoran Gallery of Art, Washington

*"At the time the picture was painted the great human drawing
card of Petitpas' was John Butler Yeats, the charming Irish
conversationalist, artist and philosopher, father of W.B. Yeats,
the Irish poet. . . . In the painting from left to right—Van Wyck
Brooks, J.B. Yeats, Alan Seeger, who wrote 'Rendezvous with
Death,' Dolly Sloan, [R. Snedden], Ann Squire, John Sloan,
Fred King." Sloan met Yeats in July of 1909, and within a few
months they became close friends. The painting was begun on
August 2, 1910.*

Oil on canvas, 32¼ x 26¼ in.

Inscribed at lower left: John Sloan/1911

Lent by Milwaukee Art Center, Gift of Mr. and Mrs. Donald B. Abert

Sloan first saw Isadora Duncan dance on February 15, 1911, and noted in his Diary, "Isadora as she appears on that big simple stage seems like all womanhood—she looms big as the mother of the race. A heavy solid figure, large columnar legs, a solid high belly, breasts not too full and her head seems no more important than it should be to give the body the chief place." Later he recalled, ". . . I viewed her through a mist of unshed tears. She lifted human movement to the level of the divine." The painting was begun on March 3. Later he portrayed Isadora several times in other media (see no. 97).

73 CARMINE THEATER   1912

Oil on canvas, 26 x 32 in.

Inscribed at lower right: John Sloan 1912

Lent by the Joseph H. Hirshhorn Foundation, New York

"Wistful little customers hanging around a small movie show."
Sloan's only oil painting that included an ash can, it followed
an outing "down to Bleecker and Carmine Sts. where I think
I have soaked in something to paint." (Diary, January 25,
1912). The next day he began Carmine Theater *from memory.*

74 McSORLEY'S BAR (McSORLEY'S ALE HOUSE)   1912

Oil on canvas, 26 x 32 in.

Inscribed at lower right: John Sloan

Lent by The Detroit Institute of Arts

"A favorite out of the way retreat for appreciative ale drinkers.
. . . It survived almost alone the modernizing of the saloon.
This painting was the first of several painted of McSorley's and
has been much appreciated . . . since prohibition was repealed."
Sloan recorded a visit to McSorley's on March 28, 1912.
Included in the Armory Show. (See nos. 75, 147 and 148.)

75 McSORLEY'S BACK ROOM   1912

Oil on canvas, 26 x 32 in.

Inscribed at lower left: John Sloan

Lent by the Dartmouth College Collection, Hanover

"McSorley's back room was like a sacristry. Here old John
McSorley would sit greeting old friends and philosophizing.
Women were never served, indeed the dingy walls and wood-
work looked as if women had set neither hand nor foot in the
place. Painted from pencil sketch."

76 A WINDOW ON THE STREET   1912

Oil on canvas, 26 x 32 in.

Inscribed at the lower left: John Sloan

Lent by the Bowdoin College Museum of Art, Brunswick, Hamlin Collection

*"The color theme of this canvas is, I think, in close harmony
with the subject. The sullen wistfulness of the woman whose
housekeeping was limited to one room."* On April 21, 1912,
Sloan wrote in his Diary, *"I saw a girl looking out of a window
in a rooming house opposite and tried to paint her from memory. I don't think I have it yet but will probably go on with it
tomorrow"* (see no. 77).

77 WOMAN AT THE WINDOW 1913

Pen and conté crayon, 15 1/16 x 14⅛ in.

Inscribed at lower right: John Sloan — '13

Lent by Mr. and Mrs. J. Warner Prins, New York

This subject, frequently observed by Sloan in the city, was depicted several times, including an oil (no. 76), two etchings (Morse 170 and 208), and an illustration, which appeared in Harper's Weekly, August 23, 1913.

78 RAINBOW, NEW YORK CITY 1912

Oil on canvas, 20 x 24 in.

Inscribed at lower left: John Sloan

Lent by Dr. and Mrs. James Hustead Semans, Durham

*On May 10, 1912 Sloan moved into a loft studio on the eleventh
floor of a building at Fourth Street and Sixth Avenue. Sloan
described the rooftop view of the city's skyscrapers in his Diary
on June 23. This sketch records the "cityscape" to the north,
including the tower of the Metropolitan Life, the tallest building in the world when completed in 1909.*

79 SUNDAY, WOMEN DRYING THEIR HAIR 1912

Oil on canvas, 25½ x 31½ in.

Inscribed at lower right: John Sloan

Lent by the Addison Gallery of American Art, Phillips Academy, Andover

*"Another of the human comedies which were regularly staged
for my enjoyment by the humble roof-top players of Cornelia
Street." The loft studio overlooked Cornelia Street to the west.
Sloan liked the painting: he exhibited it in the Armory Show
and returned to the composition in a lithograph of 1923.*

80 SUNDAY AFTERNOON IN UNION SQUARE   1912

Oil on canvas, 26¼ x 32¼ in.

Inscribed at lower right: John Sloan

Lent by the Bowdoin College Museum of Art, Brunswick, Hamlin Collection

*"Lavender light was in my mind." Union Square was the scene
of a large Socialist meeting on May 1, 1912, as Sloan noted
in his Diary, but by this time he quite consciously separated
his painting and his politics.*

81 RENGANESCHI'S SATURDAY NIGHT   1912

Oil on canvas, 26¼ x 32 in.

Inscribed at lower right: John Sloan 1912

Lent by the Art Institute of Chicago

*"Renganeschi's was . . . located on West Tenth Street, a stone's
throw from Jefferson Market Jail. The quality of light and
sense of the place, as well as the life of the dining room—
quite satisfactory."*

82 THE GREAT SUBWAY CONTRACTOR—THE PROMISED LOAF   1911

Black crayon and pen and ink over blue crayon, 13⅞ x 20¼ in.

Inscribed at lower left: John Sloan— 1911

Lent by the John Sloan Trust

This is one of the many drawings Sloan contributed to various socialist publications, in this case The Call.

The underdrawing in blue was meant to "drop out" when photographed for reproduction. Always concerned about the proper treatment of his drawings, especially those he was not paid for, Sloan wrote on the back of this one, to the chairman of the New York local of the Socialist party, "Comrade Gerber—I'd like you to share this with the Call—they could give it 6 cols. perhaps—you are to use it as wide as you possibly can carry it." And in the front margin, "Keep CLEAN and return to John Sloan 155 E 22."

83 NEW YORK HARBOR   1912

Lithographic crayon, 14¾ x 11¾ in.

Unsigned

Lent anonymously

84 THE UNEMPLOYED   1913

Line cut reproduction in two colors, 13¾ x 10 in.

Inscribed in design at lower left: John Sloan

Lent by the John Sloan Trust

One of four illustrations for "What is an American?"
by Honoré Willsie, appearing in the November 9, 1912,
issue of Collier's Weekly.

Satirical cover of the March 1913 issue of The Masses.
The simple, uncluttered layout of the page is an innovation of
Sloan's, who served without pay as art editor of the magazine.

85 AT THE TOP OF THE SWING   1913

Black chalk and pen and ink, 15 1/3 x 12¾ in.

Inscribed at lower right: John Sloan

Lent by the Yale University Art Gallery, New Haven, Gift of Dr. Charles E. Farr

86 THE RETURN FROM TOIL   1913

Crayon, 18⅜ x 14⅛ in.

Inscription at lower right: John Sloan—'13

Lent by Mr. and Mrs. J. Warner Prins, New York

This beautiful drawing, so full of spirit and life, was used on the cover of the May 1913 issue of The Masses.

This "bevy of boisterous girls with plenty of energy left after a hard day's work" appeared on the July 1913 cover of The Masses. *Sloan also etched a more complex version of this subject in 1915 (Morse 175).*

Crayon, 16½ x 25 in.

Inscribed at lower right: John Sloan—

Lent by the Whitney Museum of American Art, New York

Reproduced as a double page spread in the August 1913
Masses, in conjunction with "The Machine; Commonplace
Tragedy in One Act of Three Scenes (A Mere Chronicle of
Actual Events)," by Frank T. Shay, which exposed the
entrapment of prostitutes by the police and the judicial system
which condones the practice. Sloan felt very strongly about
the mistreatment of such women, whom he observed and
sketched in the night court. "I spent New Year's eve at the
'night court' in Jefferson Market, the women's court where
women are on the basis of their being separate cattle treated
'special.' "

88 THE HOT SPELL IN NEW YORK   1913

Crayon, 19⅞ x 25⅞ in.

Inscribed at lower left: John Sloan—

Lent by the John Sloan Trust

This drawing appeared as a double page spread in the September 6, 1913, issue of Harper's Weekly, *then under the new editorship of Norman Hapgood. The couple dancing the Turkey Trot at the left is Robert Henri and his wife, Marjorie.*

89 INNOCENT GIRLISH PRATTLE—PLUS ENVIRON-
MENT   1913

Line cut reproduction in two colors, 13¾ x 10 in.

Inscribed in design at lower right: John Sloan—13

Lent by the John Sloan Trust

90 PLAYING TO EMPTY SEATS   1913

Pencil and watercolor, 22½ x 16¼ in.

Inscribed at lower left: John Sloan

Lent by Mr. and Mrs. Arthur G. Altschul, New York

The cover of the November 1913 Masses. *The innocent girlish prattle was (in the subtitle): "What! Him? The little — — — — —! He's worse 'n she is, the — — —!"*

This drawing appeared as an independent, full page illustration in the December 6, 1913, Harper's Weekly.

91 CALLING THE CHRISTIAN BLUFF   1914

Black crayon, 19 x 28 in.

Inscribed at lower right: John Sloan 1914

Lent by Dr. and Mrs. Martin Cherkasky, New York

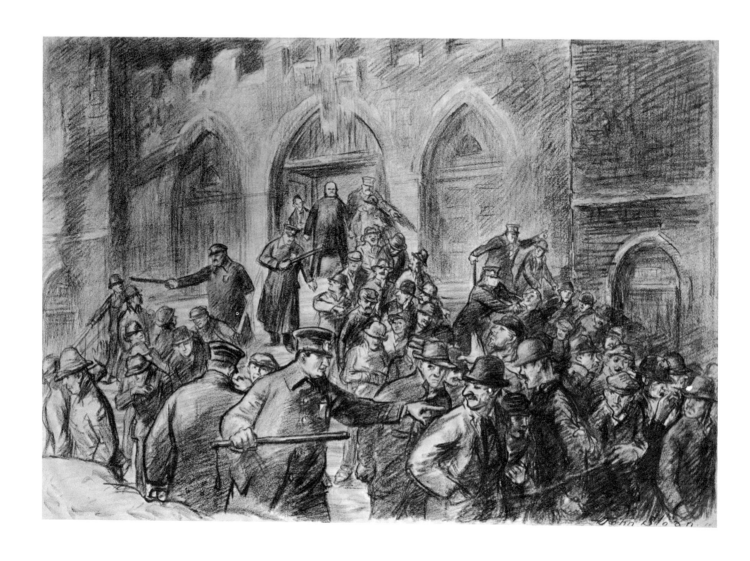

This appeared as a double page spread in the April 1914
Masses, *illustrating an article, "The Church and the Unem-*
ployed," describing a demonstration in New York on March 4.
"On that evening several hundred unemployed, most of them
homeless and all of them hungry, marched from Rutgers Square
to St. Alphonsus' church, and entered, demanding food and
shelter. They were refused . . . and ordered out of the church.
Those who did not were arrested and thrown into jail."

92 CLASS WAR IN COLORADO 1914

Black crayon, 17⅜ x 11¾ in.

Inscribed at lower right: John Sloan

Lent by the Dartmouth College Collection, Hanover

93 BACHELOR GIRL 1915

Black crayon and wash, 13½ x 13 in.

Inscribed at lower left: John Sloan—15

Lent by the Art Institute of Chicago

This powerful drawing appeared on the June 1914 cover of
The Masses, *a moving indictment of the violent repression of
a miners' strike in Colorado*

Published in the February 1915 issue of The Masses.

94 THE CONSTABULARY, POLICING THE RURAL DISTRICTS IN PHILADELPHIA, 1910   1915

Crayon and ink, 18⅝ x 25¼ in.

Inscribed at lower right: John Sloan/15

Lent by the John Sloan Trust

This drawing appeared as a double page spread in the April 1915 Masses. *The caption was: "'We need a constabulary in this state to police the rural districts'—tactful New York gentlemen. 'The proposed New York State Constabulary is modeled after that of Pennsylvania, which proved its usefulness so notably in the great street-car strike in Philadelphia'—candid Pennsylvania editor." In the background is the Philadelphia City Hall.*

95 MODEL DRESSING   c. 1913

Sanguine, 13⅛ x 8 in. (mat opening)

Inscribed in ink at lower left: John Sloan

Lent by the John Sloan Trust

96 DANCER   1915

Sanguine, 10⅝ x 8⅜ in. (mat opening)

Inscribed in pencil at lower left: John Sloan/Dec. 1915

Lent by the John Sloan Trust

This is probably a drawing of Grace Emerson, a dancer of the period whom Sloan admired. He also painted two pictures of her (Sloan estate), one dated 1917.

97 ISADORA   1915

Monotype in red-brown ink, 7⅞ x 8¾ in.

Inscribed in the design at lower left: ISADORA; and at lower right: J.S. 3/15; and in pencil at lower right margin: John Sloan

Lent by the John Sloan Trust

98 MODEL POSING ON THE COUCH   c. 1915

Black crayon, 8¾ x 14¼ in. (mat opening)

Unsigned

Lent by the John Sloan Trust

One of several depictions of the famous Isadora Duncan which Sloan did in various media (see no. 72). This monotype was done at the time of her American visit soon after the start of World War I and the tragic death of her two children. Sloan also did an etching of the dancer the same year (Morse 172). "She was quite heavy but still beautiful. A great dancer, she would bring tears to my eyes."

99 PRONE NUDE 1912

Oil on canvas, 26 x 32 in.
Inscribed at lower left: John Sloan
Lent by the John Sloan Trust

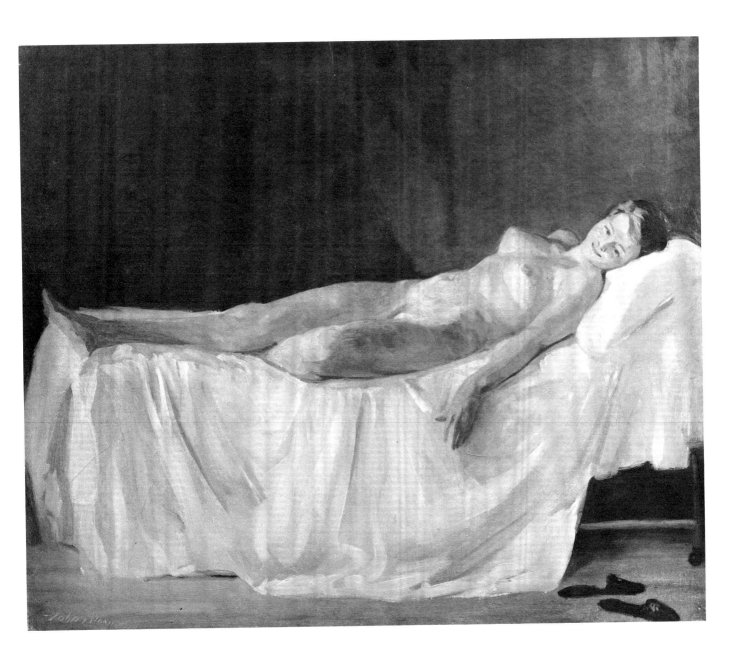

Shortly after Sloan took possession of the loft studio on Sixth Avenue in May 1912, he began his first series of paintings from the nude. His earlier studios in New York had been too cramped for figure work.

100 STUART DAVIS   1913

Oil on canvas, 32 x 26 in.

Unsigned

Lent by Mrs. Casimir B. Mayshark, Santa Fe

*Stuart Davis, the son of Sloan's old Philadelphia friend E.W.
Davis, entered the Henri class (at Sloan's urging) in 1909.
In 1913, when the portrait was painted, he was nineteen, and
a capable artist. He was represented in the Armory Show
and remained in close touch with Sloan, contributing drawings
to* The Masses.

101 THE NEW BLUE DRESS (MISS HART)   1913

Oil on canvas, 24 x 20 in.

Inscribed at lower right: John Sloan—13

Lent by the Joseph H. Hirshhorn Collection, New York

*In his figure studies of 1912 and 1913, Sloan developed a
simplified, graphic approach, reflecting the directness of his
Masses drawings.*

102 BACKYARDS, GREENWICH VILLAGE   1914

Oil on canvas, 26 x 32 in.

Inscribed at lower left: John Sloan/1914

Lent by the Whitney Museum of American Art, New York

"During the period when I occupied the studio in the loft building on Sixth Avenue, my wife and I lived in a small apartment in the neighborhood overlooking these yards." His most famous characterization of the back yard scene, *"painted from memory after careful observation of material."* A pencil sketch of the scene survives in the Sloan estate, and it presumably dates from the period prior to his move from 61 Perry Street to 240 W. 4th Street (February, 1913).

103 RED PAINT MILL   1914

Oil on canvas, 26 x 32 in.

Inscribed at lower right: John Sloan

Lent by Jo Ann and Julian Ganz, Jr., Los Angeles

"My first summer in Gloucester afforded the first opportunity
for continuous work in landscape, and I really made the most
of it." Sloan had painted almost no large landscapes since going
to New York in 1904, but he painted some seventy canvases in
Gloucester in 1914. The Red Paint Mill *is one of the most firmly*
structured; many of the others show the free brushwork that
came to climax in the painting of 1915.

104 TWIN LIGHTS—PURPLE ROCKS   1915

Oil on canvas, 26 x 32 in.

Inscribed at lower left: John Sloan

Lent by the John Sloan Trust

Sloan's experiments with a freely brushed, calligraphic approach came to a head in such canvases as this, in the summer of 1915. His admiration for the work of van Gogh, with its combination of heightened color and calligraphy, is recalled by these paintings.

105 WONSON'S ROCKS AND TEN POUND ISLAND   1915

Oil on canvas, 20 x 24 in.

Inscribed at lower right: John Sloan

Lent by the John Sloan Trust

Fluent, spontaneous, high-keyed—a glowing example of his
work of 1914-15, which incorporated the first impact of the
Armory Show. (See also the heightened movement in such
graphic works of 1915 as nos. 96 and 97.)

106 APPLE TREE   1915

Oil on canvas, 20 x 24 in.

Inscribed at lower left: John Sloan

Lent by the John Sloan Trust

*"Working from nature gives, I believe, the best means of
advance in color and spontaneous design."*

107 GLOUCESTER HARBOR 1916

Oil on canvas, 26 x 32 in.
Inscribed at lower right: John Sloan
Lent by the Syracuse University Art Collection

*"Painted from Gloucester's tallest building at that time. I think
it was four stories high. . . . A very clear memory of neutraled
crimsons and blues and warm grays."* Beginning in 1916, Sloan
placed renewed emphasis on the geometric organization of his
paintings, which became less calligraphic, more planar.

145

108 RED ROCK AND QUIET SEA   1916

Oil on canvas, 26 x 32 in.

Inscribed at lower left: John Sloan

Lent by Miss Ruth Martin, New York

"I have a distinct memory of that long straight edge of the ocean
at the horizon. The sea so quiet that it seemed like a great blue
wall. The red granite rocks were at a slant and sharp and tiring
to the feet. Plenty of patient persistence on the painter's part."
The most severe of his Gloucester compositions.

109 REDDY ON THE ROCKS   1917

Oil on canvas, 26 x 32 in.

Inscribed at lower left: John Sloan

Lent by Miss Ruth Martin, New York

*Sloan's interest in strongly geometric structure carried on into
his work of 1917, as the blocklike forms of this picture show.*

110 HILL, MAIN STREET, GLOUCESTER 1917

Oil on canvas, 26 x 32 in.

Inscribed at lower right: John Sloan

Lent by the Parrish Art Museum, Southampton

"Down this picturesque dip into town rolls a blue Mercedes,
a few years old but full of pep and power. The driver is Randall
Davey who painted in Gloucester several summers. The picture
is rich in tone and was painted on the spot." The Sloan's friendship with the Daveys led to their going together to Santa Fe
in 1919, a trip which opened new periods for both painters.

111 GLOUCESTER TROLLEY   1917

Oil on canvas, 26 x 32 in.

Inscribed at lower left: John Sloan

Lent by the Canajoharie Library and Art Musuem

"The trolleys from Rocky Neck are gone now, busses have replaced them. . . . But the little woman and Reddy in the foreground went to town long ago." The "little woman," of course was Dolly, and "Reddy" was the neighbor boy who was a favorite summer model (See no. 109).

112 MY WIFE IN BLUE   1917

Oil on canvas, 45 x 36 in.

Inscribed at lower left: John Sloan

Lent by the Museum of New Mexico, Santa Fe, Gift of Miss
Amelia Elizabeth White

"My hardest working model. In our little parlor in the red house
at Gloucester she sat without a rest for five hours in the first
pose for this portrait. . . . This is a good portrait and a good
piece of painting. Who's going to say it here if I do not?" The
picture is built up through carefully adjusted color planes.

113 JEFFERSON MARKET, SIXTH AVENUE   1917 and 1922

Oil on canvas, 32 x 26 in.

Lent by the Pennsylvania Academy of the Fine Arts,
Philadelphia

*"From 1914 to 1927 my studio on Washington Place at Sixth
Avenue provided this view to the north, with the old Jefferson
Market overlooking the Sixth Avenue elevated. . . . The painting
might be called a study in red and red-orange, and was painted
from my studio window." The Jefferson Market, with its
picturesque massing, was a motif Sloan used several times
(see nos. 117 and 149). This canvas underwent a limited
reworking in the shadow area in 1922.*

151

114 HELL HOLE 1917

Etching and aquatint, 8 x 10 in.

Inscribed in pencil at lower left: 100 proofs/Hell Hole; and at lower right: John Sloan

Lent by the John Sloan Trust

(Morse 186)

"*The back room of Wallace's at Sixth Avenue and West Fourth Street was a gathering place for artists, writers, and bohemians of Greenwich Village. The character in the upper right hand corner of the plate is Eugene O'Neill.*" *Nicknamed "the Hell Hole," this popular hangout was actually "The Golden Swan."*

115 THE RED LANE   1918

Oil on canvas, 32 x 26 in.

Inscribed at lower right: John Sloan

Lent by Mr. and Mrs. Julian P. Brodie, New York

"A quiet wagon road, muddy and red, between willows beside a pond in East Gloucester. Directly painted. The composition quite natural." Like many of the later Gloucester pictures, this reflects Sloan's concern with resistance of visual perspective in the foreground.

116 BIG APPLE TREE 1918

Oil on canvas, 32 x 26 in.

Inscribed at lower left: John Sloan

Lent anonymously

*The heavily sculptured forms of this picture stand in contrast
to the more calligraphic handling of the 1915 Apple Tree (no.
106). The painting anticipates Sloan's reinforcements of form
through texture in his work of the thirties.*

117 STEIN AT STUDIO WINDOW, SIXTH AVENUE   1918

Oil on canvas, 23 x 27 in.

Inscribed at lower right: John Sloan

Lent by the John Sloan Trust

Another version of the view north from the Washington Place studio. A comparison of this picture with Jefferson Market, Sixth Avenue (no. 113) gives an insight into Sloan's procedures of composition.

118 BLOND NUDE, ROSE SCARF   1918

Oil on canvas, 24 x 20 in.

Inscribed at lower right: John Sloan

Lent by Dr. and Mrs. Harold Rifkin, Bronx

"This is a beautiful canvas. The tonal relations are fine. If designing the figure today I would use more foreshortening in the legs. Other times, other manners." This painting foreshadows the sustained figure studies of the mid-twenties and Sloan's intense preoccupation with such subjects during the thirties.

119 GWENDOLYN   c. 1918

Oil on canvas, 24 x 20 in.

Inscribed at lower left: John Sloan

Lent by the National Collection of Fine Arts, Smithsonian Institution, Washington

Sloan was very fond of children, but he did not use them
frequently as models except during his summers at Gloucester
(1914-18).

120 RANGE AND THE BURRO 1919

Oil on canvas, 20 x 24 in.

Inscribed at lower right: John Sloan

Lent anonymously

*From 1919 to 1950, Sloan spent every summer but one at
Santa Fe. "I like to paint the landscape in the Southwest because of the fine geometrical formations and the handsome
color. Study of the desert forms, so severe and clear in that
atmosphere, helped me work out principles of plastic design,
the low relief concept. I like the colors out there. The ground is
not covered with green mold as it is elsewhere. The piñon trees
dot the surface of hills and mesas with exciting textures. . . .
Because the air is so clear you feel the reality of the things in
the distance."*

121 MOTHER AND DAUGHTER, SANTA FE   1919

Oil on canvas, 20 x 24 in.

Inscribed at lower right: John Sloan

Lent by the John Sloan Trust

*During his first summers in the Southwest Sloan was much
interested in portraying the spirit of its Mexican culture, with
its Spanish overtones, as well as the surviving customs of the
Indians.*

159

122 ROMANY MARIE   1920

Oil on canvas, 24 x 20 in.

Inscribed at lower left: John Sloan

Lent by the Whitney Museum of American Art, New York

*"Greenwich Village's famous hostess, philosopher, and friend.
This portrait like most such painted first for the painter, only
just got by with the sitter. The animation and dynamic personality of Marye would baffle a better portraitist than I." (Sloan's
spelling of "Marye" was a personal eccentricity.)*

123 CORPUS CHRISTI PROCESSION, SANTA FE 1920

Oil on canvas, 26 x 35 in.

Inscribed at lower left: John Sloan

Lent anonymously

*"A group of girls from the church orphanage passing a tem-
porary altar by the side of Camino Delgado in the annual procession early in June."* Sloan, who never traveled abroad, was
fascinated to discover the age-old traditions of the Southwest.
He projected himself into the life there with full sympathy
and respect.

161

124 PICNIC ON THE RIDGE   1920

Oil on canvas, 26 x 35 in.

Inscribed at lower right: John Sloan

Lent by Mr. and Mrs. Louis H. Aricson, Philadelphia

"*Mahonri Young, the Biesels, the Shusters, Myra Thomas,
Martha Simpson, Lois Wright, Mae Larsen, O. Wells, two
pups, many hot dogs, and an old gray Ford, a couple of miles
out on the North Road.*"

125 EAGLES OF TESUQUE   1921

Oil on canvas, 26 x 34 in.

Inscribed at lower right: John Sloan

Lent by the Colorado Springs Fine Arts Center

"*Within nine miles of a Europeanized city, for three hundred
years the little Pueblo of Tesuque has made a noble fight
against combined poverty and civilization.*" *During his first
summers in Santa Fe, Sloan traveled widely to observe Indian
ceremonies, finding "the Indian's deep harmony with all nature"
unforgettable. He was also instrumental in arranging for
exhibitions of Indian art in New York City.*

126 DANCE AT COCHITI PUEBLO, NEW MEXICO 1922

Oil on canvas, 22 x 30 in.

Inscribed at lower right: John Sloan

Lent by the John Sloan Trust

"This ceremonial Corn Dance of the Cochiti Indians brings a large crowd to the Pueblo. The horsemen on the right are visiting Navajos."

127 EAST AT SUNSET   1921

Pastel, 7⅛ x 9⅞ in. (mat opening)

Inscribed at lower left: East at Sunset Santa Fe;
and at lower right: John Sloan

Lent by the John Sloan Trust

*Study for a painting of the same title (Sloan estate), from a
sketch book. This depicts the view of the Sangre de Christo
mountains seen from the tower Sloan built next to his Santa Fe
studio. The building in the foreground was the artist's house.*

128 SANDIA MOUNTAINS,
ALBUQUERQUE, NEW MEXICO   1924

Pencil, 9⅛ x 17¼ in. (paper)
Inscribed with various color notations and at lower left: John
Sloan, 1924 / page from sketchbook; and at lower middle:
Sandia Mountains, Albuquerque, N.M.
Lent by the John Sloan Trust

129 JOHN ARMSTRONG PLAYS THE FIDDLE 1920

Crayon and pen and ink, 11⅞ x 11½ in.

Inscribed at lower right: John Sloan (paper)

Lent by the John Sloan Trust

*One of forty-seven illustrations for Edgar Lee Masters' novel,
Mitch Miller. "Vangy sat down to the organ, and John tuned up
his fiddle, and they started. Aunt Caroline came in then and
sat down and began to knit, but didn't say nothin'. John just
drew a few times with his bow and then he said: 'This here is
called 'Pete McCue's Straw Stack. . . .''"*

166

130 THE CHEATED MATE   1922

Pencil on tissue paper, 13 x 12 in. (mat opening)

Unsigned

Lent by the John Sloan Trust

131 THE CHEATED MATE   1922

Brush and ink on scratch board, 12½ x 12¼ in. (mat opening)

Inscribed at lower left: J S

Lent by the John Sloan Trust

Preliminary study for no. 131.

A finished drawing done in Sloan's wood engraving manner ("gravings on cardboard") to illustrate the poem by Milton Raison in "Sea Moods and Sea Men," published in Century Magazine, *April 1922*

The Captain was so deadly drunk,
He wanted to caress a wave,
And so they strapped him to his bunk
And left him there to rave.

The mate, who wished the captain died,
So his command the ship would be,
Thought that the captain, if untied,
Would jump into the sea.

He loosed the cords that held him down.
The captain, though, was crazy-strong
And as he climbed the rail to drown,
He took the mate along.

132 THE CITY FROM GREENWICH VILLAGE, I   c. 1922

Pencil on tissue paper, 8 x 9⅞ in. (paper)

Unsigned

Lent by the National Gallery of Art, Washington,
  Gift of Helen Farr Sloan

133 THE CITY FROM GREENWICH VILLAGE, II   c. 1922

Pencil, 9¼ x 9⅞ in. (paper)

Unsigned

Lent by the National Gallery of Art, Washington,
  Gift of Helen Farr Sloan

*This is probably the first sketch for the oil (no. 135) of the same
subject.*

Another, more developed study for the oil (no. 135).

134 THE CITY FROM GREENWICH VILLAGE, III   c. 1922

Red pencil, 8 x 10 in.

Unsigned

Lent by the National Gallery of Art, Washington,
Gift of Helen Farr Sloan

This is the most complete and detailed of the four drawings of
this subject (another appears on the back of this sheet). Since it
differs in composition from the oil (no. 135), this may have been
a preparatory study for an etching, which Sloan never did.

Oil on canvas, 26 x 34 in.

Inscribed at lower left: John Sloan

Lent by the National Gallery of Art, Washington, Gift of Helen Farr Sloan

"*Looking south over lower Sixth Avenue from the roof of my Washington Place studio, on a winter evening. The distant lights of the great office buildings downtown are seen in the gathering darkness. The triangular loft building on the right had contained my studio for three years before. Although painted from memory it seems thoroughly convincing in its handling of light and space. . . . The picture makes a record of the beauty of the older city which is giving way to the chopped-out towers of modern New York. Pencil sketch provided details.*" The painting is a culmination of Sloan's city views. It presents an extraordinary synthesis of the Village and lower Manhattan (with the Singer and Woolworth Buildings glowing on the horizon). The composition is carried far beyond the sketches, and the paint is applied with a quiet richness that anticipates Sloan's later use of glazes.

136 THRESHING FLOOR, SANTA FE   1924/25

Oil on canvas, 30 x 40 in.

Inscribed at lower right: John Sloan

Lent by the John Sloan Trust

"Within the limits of the ancient city until recently, this primitive process could be seen each autumn. A herd of goats was driven in circular stampede around a level floor of sunbaked mud."

171

137 CHAMA RUNNING RED 1925

Oil on canvas, 30 x 40 in.

Inscribed lower right: John Sloan

Lent by Miss Ruth Martin, New York

"The river is running like pink tomato soup down to the Rio
Grande and the Gulf of Mexico, carrying off the good red earth."
Undoubtedly the best-known of Sloan's Southwest landscapes.

138 RIO GRANDE COUNTRY   1925

Oil on canvas, 30 x 36 in.

Inscribed at lower right: John Sloan

Lent by the John Sloan Trust

*In several paintings of the twenties—figures, city views and
landscapes—Sloan combined firmness and clarity of structure
with breadth and even grandeur of concept.*

173

139 MODEL LEANING ON CUSHIONS, BACK TO WALL
1924

Black crayon, 8⅞ x 11⅞ in. (paper)

Inscribed in pencil at lower right: John Sloan / 24

Lent by the John Sloan Trust

140 MODEL LEANING ON LEFT HAND   1924

Pencil, 8⅞ x 11⅞ in. (paper)

Inscribed at lower left: J.S. 1924

Lent by the John Sloan Trust

Sloan's many drawings of the female figure display a wonderful diversity of styles, as he was always searching for fresh ways to depict the nude.

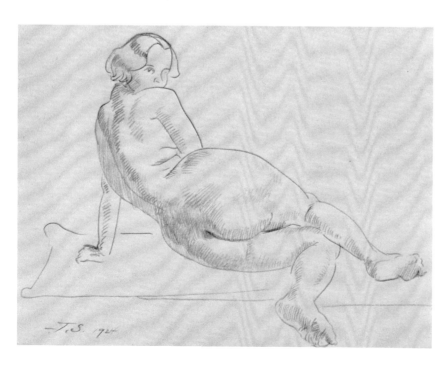

174

141 MODEL LEANING ON LEFT ELBOW   c. 1925

Pencil, 9⅞ x 12⅜ in. (paper)

Unsigned

Lent by the John Sloan Trust

142 NUDE GLANCING BACK   1926

Oil on canvas, 32 x 26 in.

Inscribed at lower left: John Sloan

Lent by Miss Ruth Martin, New York

"Well painted and well designed and the sense of surface real-
ization is quite thorough. The glance of the single eye from
under the dark hair is an amusing incident." During the mid-
twenties Sloan began to work increasingly, and with increasing
mastery, on studies of the figure.

143 DANCER WITH GREEN APPLE   c. 1927

Oil on panel, 25 x 23 in.

Unsigned

Lent by the John Sloan Trust

"Among all the racial strains we have in this country, the Negro furnishes the most beautiful individuals. They are well termed 'colored people' and more artists might find them a rich field for color-sculptural study."

144 LARGE WHITE NUDE   1927 and 1928

Oil on canvas, 30 x 40 in.

Inscribed at lower right: John Sloan

Lent anonymously

*"Painting the Irish milk-white body complexion, a whiteness
that occurs, so far as I know, in no other race, places many
difficulties in the way of exact color sculpture."* One of the most
monumental of the nudes of the series, painted just before Sloan
turned to underpainting and glaze.

145 SNOWSTORM IN THE VILLAGE   1925

Etching, 7 x 5 in. (plate)

Inscribed in pencil at lower left: 100 proofs; and at lower right: John Sloan

Lent by the John Sloan Trust
(Morse 216)

This view of the Jefferson Market Court, seen from his studio window, was a favorite of the artist's (see nos. 113 and 117).

146 14th STREET, THE WIGWAM   1928

Etching, 9¾ x 7 in. (plate)

Inscribed in pencil at lower left: 100 proofs; and at lower right: John Sloan

Lent by the John Sloan Trust
(Morse 235)

"Old Tammany Hall, the headquarters of the bosses of New York City, has ceased to exist. It lurked, menacing, in dingy red brick, facing the tawdry amusements of East Fourteenth Street." Sloan depicted this subject in oil three times, one painting being a copy of the etching done for the Federal Art Project (The Metropolitan Museum of Art).

147 McSORLEY'S CATS   1928 and 1929

Tempera with overglaze on canvas, 35 x 45 in.

Inscribed at lower left: John Sloan

Lent by the John Sloan Trust

"A drawing of this old bar made for Norman Hapgood's
Harper's Weekly helped me to produce this painting. It is
underpainted and glazed and essays a richer, deeper tone than
other McSorley subjects up to this date. The characters at the
table, left foreground, are Hippolyte Havel, Art Young, George
O. Hamlin, and J. S. . . ."

148 McSORLEY'S SATURDAY NIGHT   1929-30, 1948

Oil with overglaze on canvas, 30 x 36 in.

Inscribed at lower right: John Sloan

Lent by the Joseph H. Hirshhorn Foundation, New York

From 1928 to 1930, Sloan worked on three versions of
McSorley's, a subject he had first painted in 1912. This is the
last of the series, and is finished with linear overglaze.

149 SPRING, WASHINGTON SQUARE   1928 and 1950

Tempera and oil with overglaze on canvas, 26 x 32 in.

Inscribed at lower right: John Sloan

Lent anonymously

"For eight years my studio overlooked Washington Square. . . .
This picture . . . represents a transition between direct painting
and the 'mixed technique.' It was started in pale, neutral tones
and then worked up with more positive colors—with some
glazing in the final work." Sloan returned to the painting in
1950, almost completely repainting it and strengthening the
color tonality.

150 NUDE, RED HAIR, STANDING   1928

Oil with overglaze on panel, 28 x 20 in.

Inscribed at lower left: John Sloan

Lent anonymously

*One of the earliest figure studies in underpainting and glaze,
very freely painted. Sloan's first experiments in glaze resulted
in bold textures and colors, and a new sense of energy in his
painting.*

151 BLOND NUDE AND FLOWERS   1929

Oil with overglaze on panel, 18 x 24 in.

Inscribed at lower left: John Sloan

Lent by the John Sloan Trust

*"Here again is a rather charming color-plastic result heavily
underpainted in oil with cobalt drier and glazed two days later
with varnish medium. Note how the far leg has been increased
in size and visibility."*

Oil with overglaze on canvas, 24 x 48 in.

Inscribed at lower right: John Sloan

Lent anonymously

"*A very complete panel in which little use is made of the linear technique except in turning from the light. This is a decided variation from our general principle which calls for the lines as color-textural definition of the lightened surface. . . . The increase in volume of the far side of the figure is very successful because quite unnoticeable.*" Of a companion picture (Nude, Four Senses, 1929) Sloan remarked, "*A student may easily observe the relationship to the technique of tradition by way of Renoir.*"

185

153 MODEL READING NEWSPAPER   1930

Pencil on tissue paper, 9⅞ x 13⅞ in. (paper)

Inscribed along left side (under mat): NYC Nov 1930 J.S.

Lent by the John Sloan Trust

154 NUDE ON STAIRS 1930

Etching, 10 x 8 in. (plate)

Inscribed in pencil at lower left: 100 proofs; and at lower right: John Sloan

Lent by the John Sloan Trust

(Morse 241)

*One of Sloan's first etched nudes, and one of the most monumentally
conceived, with rich blackness in the complex line work.*

155 ROBERT HENRI, PAINTER   1931

Etching, 14 x 11 in. (plate) 7th state

Inscribed at lower left: John Sloan—31; and at lower center: Robert Henri, Painter

Lent by the John Sloan Trust

(Morse 246)

Sloan always acknowledged the importance of Henri's friendship, guidance and encouragement on his development as an artist. Speaking of this particular etching, Sloan stated, "Made after his death, from a planned portrait sketch of twenty-five years before. I am pleased with the plate and hope that it conveys some of the kindly strength and helpful wisdom which this great artist so freely gave to others." The portrait sketch, dated 1905, is in the collection of the University of Nebraska. In 1904 Sloan etched a similar portrait of Henri, but canceled the plate after two or three proofs.

156 NUDE ON CHAISE LONGUE BY WINDOW 1933

Etching, 6 x 11½ in. (plate)

Inscribed in pencil at lower left: 100 proofs; and at lower right: John Sloan

Lent by the John Sloan Trust

(Morse 273)

157 BRUNETTE NUDE, STRIPED BLANKET   1928 and 1930

Oil on canvas, subsequently glazed, 26 x 32 in.

Inscribed at upper right: John Sloan

Lent by Miss Ruth Martin, New York

As Sloan developed his personal technique of glaze reinforced
with linework, he carried his "realization" of form to the point
at which it began to take on the tactile impact of sculpture.

158 JUANITA 1930

Tempera with overglaze on panel, 32 x 26 in.

Inscribed at upper left: John Sloan

Lent anonymously

*"Charming example of the pretty girl of an old family in Santa
Fe.... She might properly have been given more delicacy, but
I was interested more in her vigorous youth." Once again, the
figure achieves a sculptured monumentality. When the form
of the flesh achieved solidity without linear overglaze, Sloan
applied it sparingly if at all.*

159 VAGIS, THE SCULPTOR 1930

Tempera with overglaze on panel, 24 x 30 in.

Inscribed at lower right: John Sloan

Lent by the John Sloan Trust

*"When a news agency asked for a photograph of this picture
informing me that it had been awarded a portrait prize, I told
them there must be some mistake, that I did not paint portraits.
. . . That it should be . . . condemned to a prize on those grounds
was most surprising. Strong color-textural accompaniment to
volume and graphic vitality."*

160 GIRL, BACK TO THE PIANO   1932
Tempera with overglaze on panel, 20 x 24 in.
Inscribed at lower left: John Sloan
Lent by the John Sloan Trust

*"An excellent color tonal quality pervades this canvas. The
linear texture comes and goes, here and there, and is perhaps
on that account very satisfactory. The nature of the light is well
expressed."*

193

161 MODEL IN DRESSING ROOM   1933

Tempera with overglaze on panel, 36 x 30 in.

Inscribed at lower left: John Sloan

Lent by the Whitney Museum of American Art, New York

"A sense of ripening begins to pervade me. I am sixty-two years old, almost ready to study abroad. . . . This is a painting that proves I am going somewhere." The amount of linear overglaze varied from painting to painting during the thirties; here it is practically absent.

162 LOOKING OUT ON WASHINGTON SQUARE   1933

Tempera with overglaze on panel, 36 x 30 in.

Inscribed at lower right: John Sloan

Lent anonymously

For over thirty years, Sloan summered in Santa Fe, but in 1933 he remained in New York City. "A summer indoors in a big, high-ceilinged studio . . . overlooking Washington Square and the arch at the end of Fifth Avenue. Children dabbled like ducks in the pool around the fountain almost under my win- *dow; the busses picked up hundreds to ride up Riverside Drive, teeming, stewing life below me; coolness, peace, and plenty of work; a memorable summer indoors." The studio, which Sloan occupied from 1927 to 1935, appears again in no. 164, and the view from the window in no. 149.*

163 PORTRAIT (AMELIA ELIZABETH WHITE)   1934

Tempera with overglaze on panel, 36 x 24 in.

Inscribed at lower left: John Sloan

Lent by the Whitney Museum of American Art, New York

Gift of Miss Amelia Elizabeth White

"My sitter asserts her liking for this picture which to my mind
rates her high in ability to look on a picture as created work."
Miss White was long a close friend of the Sloans, working with
them in support of American Indian art and serving as a staunch
patron of the artist.

Tempera with overglaze on panel, 36 x 23 in.

Inscribed at lower right: John Sloan '35

Lent anonymously

"The writer and artist frankly admits a strong personal liking for this picture. It is a record of our home life in the studio. The cat on the balustrade is a figment of the imagination. The picture has power, and the problems of chiaroscuro are well met. Its departure from visual representation is much greater than is apparent. It was painted by daylight and from memory in the studio which was the setting."

197

165 NUDE AND NINE APPLES 1937

Tempera with overglaze on panel, 24 x 30 in.

Inscribed at lower left: John Sloan—37

Lent by the Whitney Museum of American Art, New York

"*Every good picture leaves the painter eager to start again,
unsatisfied, inspired by the rich mine in which he is working;
hoping for more energy, more vitality, more time—condemned
to painting for life.*" *The picture culminates ten years of figure
work in underpainting and glaze.*

166 JEANNE DUBINSKY 1940/42

Tempera with overglaze on panel, 30 x 24 in.

Inscribed at upper left: John Sloan

Lent by the John Sloan Trust

*Ill health interfered with Sloan's production of paintings during
the early forties. Only a few works such as this—and a portrait
of the sitter's father, David Dubinsky—date from the period.
"One of the most important of my paintings, full of graphic
sculptural power."*

199

167 RIDERS IN THE HILLS   1946

Tempera with overglaze on panel, 19⅝ x 20 in.

Inscribed at lower left: John Sloan 46

Lent by the Whitney Museum of American Art, New York,

Gift of Mrs. John Sloan

A small painting, but with the sparkling clarity that was to characterize much of the work of Sloan's last six years.

168 SELF-PORTRAIT (PIPE AND BROWN JACKET)   1946 and 1947

Tempera with overglaze on panel, 16 x 12 in.

Inscribed at lower right: John Sloan 46

Lent anonymously

*Sloan at seventy-five, his health recovered, was alert, vigorous
and in full control of his powers as a painter. Note that in such
paintings as this he held back on linear texturing when forms
came through strongly without it.*

169 THE GREEN DANCE DRESS (THE DANCE DRESS)   1945 and 1946

Tempera with overglaze on panel, 28⅞ x 23½ in.

Inscribed at lower left: John Sloan

Lent by The Metropolitan Museum of Art, New York, Bequest of Miss Adelaide Milton deGroot, 1967

*Paintings of the last period show increased emphasis on large
shapes that fill the entire canvas.*

170 SANTA FE SIESTA   1948 and 1949, 1951

Tempera with overglaze on panel, 22 x 35 in.

Inscribed at lower left: John Sloan, '48 '9

Lent anonymously

*The emphasis shifts from the heavily sculptured individual
figures of the thirties to contained shapes that work with the
other large shapes of the painting. The tradition of the old
masters—especially the Venetians—is on Sloan's mind: note the
dog in the corner and the distant mountain.*

171 STUDY FOR REALIZATION—NUDE WITH FOOT ON BOOK   1949

Charcoal, 24⅞ x 14⅞ in. (paper)

Inscribed in pencil at lower right: John Sloan/49

Lent by the John Sloan Trust

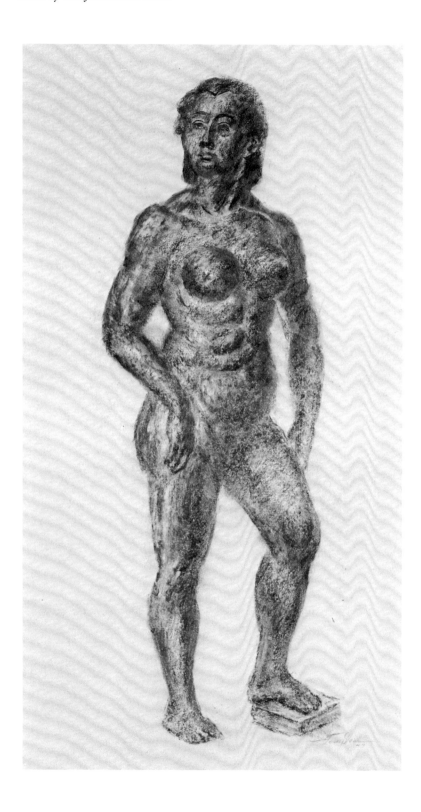

172 MONUMENT IN THE PLAZA   1948 and 1949

Tempera with overglaze on panel, 32 x 26 in.

Inscribed at lower right: John Sloan 49

Lent by the John Sloan Trust

Sloan's last, and most monumental, treatment of a favorite recurring subject,
the plaza of Santa Fe. On the bench to the left are seated John and Helen Farr Sloan.

173 TEA FOR ONE   1948 and 1950

Tempera with overglaze on panel, 32 x 26 in.

Inscribed at lower right: John Sloan '48

Lent anonymously

Helen Farr Sloan, painted at Sinagua. The white-on-white
still life reminds us that Sloan admonished his students that
"we need to do more of that kind of studying into the real
nature of form and texture. . . ."

174 LADY AND REMBRANDT   1950 and 1951

Tempera with overglaze on panel, 24 x 18 in.

Inscribed at lower left: John Sloan/50

Lent by the John Sloan Trust

Beside the Rembrandt on the mantel is Sloan's Nude at Foot of
the Stairs *(1933)—one of his favorites among his own paintings.*

175 MODEL WITH RED HAND MIRROR   1950

Tempera with overglaze on panel, 30 x 24 in.

Inscribed at lower right: John Sloan 50

Lent by the John Sloan Trust

The transformation of the "eyesight" reality to a "mind-sight"
reality is carried to a new height, with new formal order, in
Sloan's very late paintings.

Tempera on panel; unfinished, 24 x 30 in.

Unsigned

Lent anonymously

John Sloan spent his last summer at Hanover, New Hampshire,
where he began a series of landscapes. Mink Brook, *which is*
in tempera only, appears completely resolved, though intended
for glazing later.

BOOKS ILLUSTRATED BY JOHN SLOAN

KEELY, ROBERT N., JR., and G. G. DAVIS. *In Arctic Seas: The Voyage of the Kite with the Peary Expedition*. Philadelphia, Rufus C. Hartranft, 1892. 14 illustrations.

POLLARD, PERCIVAL. *Cape of Storms*. Chicago, The Echo, 1895. Frontispiece illustration (Cover design by Will H. Bradley).

WAYNE, CHARLES STOKES. *The Lady and Her Tree*. Philadelphia, The Vortex Co., 1895. Cover design.

LINDSEY, WILLIAM. *Cinder-Path Tales*. Boston, Copeland and Day, 1896. Cover design (also used as poster).

One Hundred Years: MacKellar, Smith, and Jordan Foundry. Philadelphia, privately printed, 1896. Cover design.

SNYDER, CHARLES MCCLOY. *Comic History of Greece*. Philadelphia, J. P. Lippincott Co., 1898. 27 illustrations.

CRANE, STEPHEN. *Great Battles of the World*. Philadelphia, J. P. Lippincott Co., 1901. 8 illustrations.

EDWARDS, LOUISE BETTS. *The Tu-Tze's Tower*. Philadelphia, Henry T. Coates, 1903. 4 illustrations.

DE KOCK, CHARLES PAUL. *Monsieur Dupont*. Boston, Frederick J. Quinby Co., 1902. Vol. 1: 1 etching, 1 illustration; Vol. 2: 2 etchings.

_____. *The Barber of Paris*. Boston, Frederick J. Quinby Co., 1903. Vol. 1: 1 illustration; Vol. 2: 1 illustration.

_____. *Frère Jacques*. Boston, Frederick J. Quinby Co., 1903. Vol. 1: 1 etching, 1 illustration; Vol. 2: 3 etchings.

_____. *The Gogo Family*. Boston, Frederick J. Quinby Co., 1903. Vol. 1: 4 etchings, 1 illustration; Vol. 2: 2 etchings, 1 illustration.

_____. *Memoirs*. Boston, Frederick J. Quinby Co., 1903. 2 etchings.

_____. *Adhémar*. Boston, Frederick J. Quinby Co., 1904. 5 etchings, 6 illustrations.

_____. *André the Savoyard*. Boston, Frederick J. Quinby Co., 1904. Vol. 1: 3 etchings, 8 illustrations; Vol. 2: 4 etchings, 7 illustrations.

_____. *Jean*. Boston, Frederick J. Quinby Co., 1904. Vol. 2: 3 etchings, 1 illustration.

_____. *Madame Pantalon*. Boston, Frederick J. Quinby Co., 1904. 4 etchings, 6 illustrations.

_____. *Cherami*. Boston, Frederick J. Quinby Co., 1905. Vol. 1: 4 etchings, 5 illustrations; Vol. 2: 5 etchings, 5 illustrations.

_____. *Flower Girl*. Boston, Frederick J. Quinby Co., 1905. Vol. 1: 5 etchings, 5 illustrations; Vol. 2: 5 etchings, 5 illustrations.

DALY, THOMAS AUGUSTINE. *Canzoni*. Philadelphia, David McKay, 1906. 1 etching and 17 illustrations.

COLLINS, WILKIE. *The Moonstone*. New York, Charles Scribner's Sons, 1908. 4 illustrations.

_____. *The New Magdalen*. New York, Charles Scribner's Sons, 1908. 4 illustrations.

KIRKPATRICK, GEORGE R. *War, What For?* West La Fayette, Ohio, published by the author, 1910. 11 illustrations.

DALY, THOMAS AUGUSTINE. *Madrigali*. Philadelphia, David McKay, 1912. 1 etching, 11 illustrations.

GABORIAU, EMIL. *Baron Trigault's Vengeance*. New York, Charles Scribner's Sons, 1913. 4 illustrations.

_____. *Caught in the Net*. New York, Charles Scribner's Sons, 1913. 4 illustrations.

_____. *The Champdoce Mystery*. New York, Charles Scribner's Sons, 1913. 4 illustrations.

_____. *The Clique of Gold*. New York, Charles Scribner's Sons, 1913. 4 illustrations.

_____. *The Count's Millions*. New York, Charles Scribner's Sons, 1913. 4 illustrations.

_____. *Within an Inch of His Life*. New York, Charles Scribner's Sons, 1913. 4 illustrations.

REED, JOHN. *The Cook and the Captain Bold*. New York, Metropolitan Publishing Co., 1915. Cover design and 4 illustrations, reprinted from *The Metropolitan Magazine*, November 1914.

ENGLAND, GEORGE ALLEN. *The Air Trust*. St. Louis, Mo., Phil Wagner, 1915. 6 illustrations.

MASTERS, EDGAR LEE. *Mitch Miller*. New York, The Macmillan Co., 1920. Cover and 47 illustrations.

BERGENGREN, RALPH. *Gentlemen All and Merry Companions*. Boston, B. J. Brimmer Co., 1922. Cover design and 25 illustrations, reprinted from ten various issues of *Collier's* and *Everybody's Magazine* in which the stories first appeared.

RAISON, MILTON. *Spindrift*. New York, George H. Doran, 1922. 2 illustrations.

CAHILL, HOLGER. *Profane Earth*. New York, The Macaulay Co., 1927. Cover and dust jacket design.

MILLER, MAX. *The Beginning of a Mortal*. New York, E. P. Dutton, 1933. 20 illustrations.

MAUGHAM, W. SOMERSET. *Of Human Bondage*. New Haven, Limited Editions Club, 1938. 16 etchings in two volumes.

SELECTED BIBLIOGRAPHY

Publications on or by John Sloan

BROOKS, VAN WYCK, *John Sloan: A Painter's Life*, New York, 1955.

DU BOIS, GUY PÈNE, *John Sloan*, New York, 1931.

GOODRICH, LLOYD, *John Sloan*, New York, 1952 [Whitney Museum of American Art Catalogue].

HOLCOMB, GRANT, *A Checklist for John Sloan's Paintings*, Annie Halenbake Ross Library, Lock Haven, Pennsylvania, 1970.

MORSE, PETER, *John Sloan's Prints: A Catalogue Raisonné of the Etchings, Lithographs and Posters*, New Haven and London, 1969.

ST. JOHN, BRUCE, *John Sloan*, New York, 1971.

SLOAN, JOHN, *Gist of Art*, ed. Helen Farr, New York, 1939.

SLOAN, JOHN, *New York Scene: From the Diaries, Notes and Correspondence 1906-1913*, ed. Bruce St. John, introduction and notes by Helen Farr Sloan, New York, 1965.

SLOAN, JOHN, *The Poster Period of John Sloan*, ed. Helen Farr Sloan, Lock Haven, Pennsylvania, 1967.

SLOAN, JOHN AND LA FARGE, OLIVER, *Introduction to American Indian Art*, The Exposition of Indian Tribal Art, Inc., New York, 1931.

John Sloan, American Artists Group, Inc., New York, 1945.

John Sloan, edited with an introduction by A. E. Gallatin, New York, 1925.

WEST, HERBERT FAULKNER, *John Sloan's Last Summer*, Iowa City, 1952.

Articles and Introductions by John Sloan

"Art Is, Was, and Ever Will Be," in Oliver M. Sayler, *Revolt in the Arts*, New York, 1930, pp. 318-21.

"Randall Davey," *New Mexico Quarterly Review*, vol. 21 (Spring, 1951), pp. 19-25.

"The Indian as Artist," *Survey*, vol. 67 (December 1, 1931), pp. 243-46.

Introduction: William M. Thackeray, *Vanity Fair*, Heritage Press ed., New York, 1940.

Introduction to Ira Moskowitz and John Collier, *Patterns and Ceremonials of the Indians of the Southwest*, New York, 1949, pp. 5-7.

"My Recent Encounter," *Creative Art*, vol. 2 (May, 1928), Supplement, pp. XLIV-XLV.

"The Process of Etching," *Touchstone*, vol. 8 (December, 1920), pp. 227, 238-40. (Reprinted in Peter Morse, *John Sloan's Prints*, pp. 388-392.)

"A Tale of Wickedness on Wings" [Illustrated Poem], *Collier's*, vol. 46 (December 10, 1910), p. 27.

See also statements by Sloan in his exhibition catalogs, and in: The Metropolitan Museum of Art, *Robert Henri Memorial Exhibition*, 1931, pp. xi-xii; and Whitney Museum of American Art, *Juliana Force and American Art*, 1949, pp. 32-42.

Exhibition Catalogs

Addison Gallery of American Art, Phillips Academy, Andover, *John Sloan Retrospective Exhibition*, 1938, (Notes by Sloan).

American Academy of Arts and Letters and National Institute of Arts and Letters, New York, *Exhibition of Work by . . . Recipients of Honors*, 1950.

Annie Halenbake Ross Library, Lock Haven, *The Early Landscapes of John Sloan*, 1969. Comments and checklist by Grant Holcomb.

Brooklyn Museum, Brooklyn, *The Eight*, 1943-44.

Carnegie Institute, Pittsburgh, *An Exhibition of Etchings by John Sloan*, 1937.

Dartmouth College, Hanover, *John Sloan Painting and Prints* (*Seventy-fifth Anniversary Retrospective*), 1946, (Notes by Sloan).

Delaware Art Center, Wilmington, *The Fiftieth Anniversary of the Exhibition of Independent Artists in 1910*, 1960.

Hudson Guild, New York, *Exhibition of Paintings, Etchings and Drawings by John Sloan*, 1916, (Notes by Sloan).

Kraushaar Galleries, New York, *Complete Collection of Etchings by John Sloan*, 1937.

_____, *John Sloan Retrospective Exhibition*, 1948.

Lock Haven State College, Lock Haven, *The John Sloan Exhibit*, 1970.

Macbeth Galleries, New York, *Exhibition of Paintings . . .*, 1908, [The Eight].

Missouri, University of, Columbia, *A Selection of Etchings by John Sloan*, (Introduction by Peter Morse), 1967.

Museum of Modern Art, New York, *Paintings by Nineteen Living Americans*, 1929-30.

Philadelphia Museum of Art, Philadelphia, *Artists of the Philadelphia Press*, 1945, ("Artists of the Press," pp. 7-8, by John Sloan).

Renaissance Society, University of Chicago, *Retrospective Exhibition of Etchings by John Sloan*, 1945, (Notes by Sloan).

Smithsonian Institution, Washington, D. C., *John Sloan*, 1961, (Essays by Helen Farr Sloan and Bruce St. John).

Title III E.S.E.A., Area "J" (sponsor), *An Exhibition of Selected John Sloan Paintings [and Graphics]*, (Introduction and notes by Mrs. John Sloan), 1968.

Walker Art Museum, Bowdoin College, Brunswick, *The Art of John Sloan*, 1962, (essay by Philip C. Beam).

Wanamaker Galleries, New York, *Retrospective Exhibition: John Sloan Paintings, Etchings and Drawings*, 1939.

Wanamaker Galleries, Philadelphia, *Retrospective Exhibition: John Sloan, Paintings, Etchings and Drawings*, 1940.

Whitney Museum of American Art, New York, *New York Realists 1900-1914*, 1937, p. 7.

[Whitney Studio], Mrs. H. P. Whitney's Studio, New York, *Exhibition of Paintings, Etchings & Drawings by John Sloan*, 1916.

Wilmington Society of the Fine Arts, Wilmington, *The Life and Times of John Sloan*, 1961, (Essays by Helen Farr Sloan and Bruce St. John).

Books

BROWN, MILTON W., *The Story of the Armory Show*, New York, 1963.

BULLARD, E. JOHN, *John Sloan and the Philadelphia Realists as Illustrators* (Master's thesis, University of California, Los Angeles, 1968).

CAFFIN, CHARLES H., *The Story of American Painting*, New York, 1907, pp. 378-81.

CAHILL, HOLGER and BARR, ALFRED H., JR., ed., *Art in America in Modern Times*, New York, 1934, pp. 31-32.

CRAVEN, THOMAS, *Modern Art*, New York, 1934, pp. 326-28.

——————, *A Treasury of American Prints*, New York, 1939, 5 ill.

EASTMAN, MAX, *Enjoyment of Living*, New York, 1948.

——————, *Love and Revolution*, New York, 1964, pp. 492 and 600.

GALLATIN, A. E., *Certain Contemporaries*, New York, 1916, pp. 23-30.

GELDZAHLER, HENRY, *American Painting in the Twentieth Century*, New York, 1965, pp. 26-30, 224.

GLACKENS, IRA, *William Glackens and the Ashcan Group*, New York, 1957.

HOMER, WILLIAM INNES, *Robert Henri and His Circle*, Ithaca and London, 1969.

LAFOLLETTE, SUZANNE, *Art In America*, New York, 1929, pp. 304-07, 324-25.

LARKIN, OLIVER W., *Art and Life in America*, New York, 1949.

MATHER, FRANK, JEWETT, JR., "John Sloan," *American Art Portfolios*, ser. I, New York, 1936, pp. 54-58.

——————, MOREY, CHARLES RUFUS, and HENDERSON, WILLIAM JAMES, *The American Spirit in Art*, New Haven, 1927, pp. 153, 268, 317.

MELLQUIST, JEROME, *The Emergence of an American Art*, New York, 1942, pp. 42, 119, 130-34.

PERLMAN, BENNARD B., *The Immortal Eight, American Painting from Eakins to the Armory Show, 1870-1913*, with Introduction by Mrs. John Sloan, New York, 1962.

PEARSON, RALPH M., *Experiencing American Pictures*, New York, 1943, pp. 164-68.

PHILLIPS, DUNCAN, *A Collection in the Making*, New York, 1926, pp. 51-52.

POSTERS IN MINIATURE, New York, 1897.

RUEPPEL, MERRILL CLEMENT, *The Graphic Art of Arthur Bowen Davies and John Sloan*, Ann Arbor, University Microfilms, 1956.

Periodicals

"Art Students League Mourns Passing of John Sloan," *Art Students League News*, vol. 4 (October 1, 1951), pp. 1-4.

BARKER, RUTH LAUGHLIN, "John Sloan Reviews the Indian Tribal Arts," *Creative Art*, vol. 9 (December, 1931), pp. 444-49.

BARRELL, CHARLES WISNER, "The Real Drama of the Slums, as Told in John Sloan's Etchings," *The Craftsman*, vol. 15 (February, 1909), pp. 559-64.

BAURY, LOUIS, "The Message of Bohemia," *Bookman*, vol. 34 (November 1911), pp. 262-65.

BOHROD, AARON, "On John Sloan," *College Art Journal*, vol. 10 (Fall, 1950), pp. 3-9.

BRACE, ERNEST, "John Sloan," *Magazine Art*, vol. 31 (March, 1938), pp. 130-35, 183-84.

BROWN, MILTON W., "The Two John Sloans," *Art News*, vol. 50 (January, 1952), pp. 24-27, 56-57.

CAHILL, EDGAR (HOLGER), "John Sloan," *Shadowland*, vol. 4 (August, 1921), pp. 10-11, 71-73.

COATES, ROBERT M., "Profiles," *New Yorker*, vol. 25 (May 7, 1949).

"Dartmouth Shows Fifty Years of John Sloan," *Art News*, vol. 45 (August, 1946), pp. 38-39.

EDGERTON, GILES, "The Younger American Painters: Are They Creating a National Art?," *The Craftsman*, vol. 13 (February, 1908), p. 523.

ELY, CATHERINE BEACH, "The Modern Tendency in Henri, Sloan and Bellows," *Art In America,* vol. 10 (April, 1922), pp. 132-38, 143.

GUTMAN, WALTER, "John Sloan," *Art in America,* vol. 17 (June, 1929), pp. 187-95.

HENRI, ROBERT, "The New York Exhibition of Independent Artists," *The Craftsman,* vol. 18 (May, 1910), pp. 162, 168, 172.

KWIAT, JOSEPH J., "John Sloan: An American Artist as a Social Critic, 1900-1917," *Arizona Quarterly,* X, (Spring, 1954), pp. 52-64.

LARRIC, J. B., "John Sloan-Etcher," *Coming Nation,* no. 69 (January 6, 1912), pp. 3-4.

MECHLIN, LEILA, Editorial, *American Magazine of Art,* vol. 21 (May, 1930), pp. 282-83.

KATZ, LESLIE, "The World of the Eight," *Arts Yearbook,* vol. 1 (1957), pp. 55-76.

MORSE, JOHN D., "John Sloan, 1871-1951," *American Artist,* vol. 16 (January, 1952), pp. 24-28, 57-60.

MORSE, PETER, "John Sloan's Etching Technique: An Example," *Smithsonian Journal of History,* vol. 2 (1967, no. 3), pp. 17-34.

Notes, *Chap-Book,* Chicago, vol. 2 (November 15, 1894), p. 40.

PACH, WALTER, "L'Art de John Sloan," *L'Art et les Artistes,* Paris, vol. 18 (February, 1914), pp. 222-26.

_____, "Quelques notes sur les peintres americains," *Gazette des Beaux-Arts,* vol. 51 (Paris, 1909), pp. 324-35.

_____, "John Sloan," *Atlantic Monthly,* vol. 194 (August, 1954), pp. 68-72.

_____, "John Sloan," *New Mexico Quarterly Review,* vol. 19 (Summer, 1949), pp. 177-81.

_____, "John Sloan Today," *Virginia Quarterly Review,* vol. 1 (July, 1925), pp. 196-204.

PENN, F., "Newspaper Artists—John Sloan," *Inland Printer,* vol. 14 (October, 1894), p. 50.

ROBERTS, MARY FANTON, "John Sloan: His Art and Its Inspiration," *Touchstone,* vol. 4 (February, 1919), pp. 362-70.

SALPETER, HARRY, "Saturday Night's Painter," *Esquire,* vol. 5 (June, 1936), pp. 105-07, 132, 134.

"John Sloan: A Great Teacher Painter Crusades for American Art," *Life,* vol. 7 (December 11, 1939), pp. 44-46.

"John Sloan—Painter and Engraver," *Index of Twentieth Century Artists,* vol. 1, no. 11 (August, 1934), and volume 2, no. 12, supplements no. 11 and 12.

Art Students League News, vol. 3 (December 1, 1950), pp. 3-7, [Speech by John Sloan, Art Students League Diamond Jubilee Dinner].

WATSON, FORBES, "John Sloan," *Magazine of Art,* vol. 45 (1952), pp. 62-70.

WEITENKAMPF, FRANK, "John Sloan in the Print Room," *American Magazine of Art,* vol. 20 (October, 1929), pp. 554-59.

YEATS, JOHN BUTLER, "The Work of John Sloan," *Harper's Weekly,* vol. 58 (Nov. 22, 1913), pp. 20-21.

ZIGROSSER, CARL, "John Sloan Memorial: His Complete Graphic Work," *Philadelphia Museum Bulletin,* vol. 51 (Winter, 1956), pp. 19-31.

INDEX OF WORKS

75913
S634J

COPY   1

VOLUME

PART

EDITION

YEAR   1971

CONTROL NO. 771687

COST   9.95

SLOAN JOHN

JOHN SLOAN 18